The Age of Complexity
36 Children
The Open Classroom
Golden Boy as Anthony Cool: A Photo Essay on Naming and Graffiti
Reading: How to—
A People's Guide to Alternative Ways of Teaching and Testing Reading
Half the House
On Teaching
View from the Oak
Growing with Your Children
A Book of Puzzlements
Basic Skills
Growing Minds: On Becoming a Teacher
Mathematical Puzzlements
Making Theater: Developing Plays with Young People
The Question Is College
From Archetype to Zeitgeist: A Dictionary of Powerful Ideas
"I Won't Learn from You" and Other Forms of Creative Maladjustment
Should We Burn Babar
The Discipline of Hope
A Grain of Poetry
Stupidity and Tears
She Would Not Be Moved

PAINTING
CHINESE

A LIFELONG TEACHER
GAINS THE WISDOM OF YOUTH

HERBERT KOHL

BLOOMSBURY

Author's note: Some of the names, locations, and details of events
in this book have been changed to protect the privacy of persons involved.

Some Chinese names and terms are spelled using the old Wade-Giles
transliteration system, others using the Pinyin system, depending
on the source material to which the author referred.

Copyright © 2007 by Herbert Kohl

All illustrations by Herbert Kohl unless otherwise indicated.
Figures on pages 20, 21, 62, and 65 copyright © Jose Arenas.
Characters and stamp on pages 99 and 100 copyright © Joseph Zhuoqing Yan.

Published by Bloomsbury USA, New York
Distributed to the trade by Holtzbrinck Publishers

All papers used by Bloomsbury USA are natural, recyclable products made
from wood grown in well-managed forests. The manufacturing processes
conform to the environmental regulations of the country of origin.

LIBRARY OF CONGRESS CATALOGING-IN-PUBLICATION DATA
Kohl, Herbert R.
Painting Chinese : a lifelong teacher gains the wisdom of youth / Herbert Kohl.
p. cm.
Includes bibliographical references.
ISBN-10 1-59691-052-6 (alk. paper)
ISBN-13 978-1-59691-052-2 (alk. paper)
1. Kohl, Herbert R. 2. Teachers—United States—Biography. 3. Teaching. 4. Learning.
5. Aging. I. Title.
LA2317.K64A3 2007
371.10092—dc22
[B]
2006039324

First U.S. Edition 2007

1 3 5 7 9 10 8 6 4 2

Designed by Sara Stemen
Typeset by Westchester Book Group
Printed in the United States of America by Quebecor World Fairfield

To Joseph Zhuoqing Yan, Janny Xiao Qin Huang,
and the Joseph Fine Arts School

Trust your heart,
And your brush will be inspired.
Writing and painting have the same intent,
The revelation of innate goodness.
Here are two companions,
An aged tree and a tall bamboo,
Transformed by his brush,
Finished in an instant.
The embodiment of a moment
Is the treasure of hundreds of years,
And one feels, unrolling it, recognition,
As if seeing the man himself.

—T'ANG HOU (ACTIVE FOURTEENTH CENTURY)

My journey into painting Chinese was unanticipated. It began with discovering that I was becoming an old man. About four years ago, my wife, Judy, and I were in a local market buying food for dinner. As usual, I wandered off to the little section where they sold cheap toys and games and chose a bag of small plastic fire-fighters and policemen billed as a "9/11 Heroes" kit to add to my collection of painted Dungeons & Dragons figurines, nativity scenes, action figures, and other miscellaneous tchotchkes. At the checkout counter, the cashier rang up the food and the figures and asked, in a very pleasant voice, if the playthings were for my grandchildren. I was surprised.

Those days I was feeling young and creative, very much the middle-aged guy who was trying to preserve the child in himself. However, she saw me as a grandfather. I had never seen myself that way, and her casual comment troubled me.

I never experienced anxiety when I passed thirty-five, never had a middle-age crisis in my forties or fifties. I just kept on working on external things: working with children, writing, and advocating for social justice. The work I did was a source of energy and strength, and I always felt I could continue doing it at the same level and with the same intensity as long as I desired. But as I was approaching seventy, there were times when I felt old, tired, and vulnerable. After a twelve-hour day, my hip hurt and I limped. I can trace that back to an auto injury when I was twenty-seven, though I'd been pain-free for over thirty years. It was not just the pain and fatigue that led me to feel old. My wife and I had lost our parents when in our sixties and had witnessed their aging and dying. That witness was painful, and as we inherit the role of family elders, we now both see ourselves moving along the same slow path.

Recently, aging has come closer to center stage as a number of old friends have become very ill, a few have died, and a few are tenuously but stubbornly holding on to life. I see myself in them and on occasion am overwhelmed by the sense of my finitude. Sometimes I find myself surveying my toys and books and plants and wonder what will happen when I'm no longer around to care for them. The possibility that the whole fabric of my life, memories, friendships, and the working environment I have shaped so carefully over the past fifty years can dissolve in a moment is distressing.

My own children joke about my concerns about aging and, I believe, see me as I was when they were younger, just as I still see them as they were as children even though they are in their mid- and late thirties.

。 。 。

For the five years before I turned seventy, I created and directed a teacher education program at the University of San Francisco based on the idea of integrating issues of social justice throughout the curriculum, hoping to bring young idealistic people into public school teaching and to fortify them with the skills and stamina to make their dreams practical realities. I succeeded in recruiting thirty students to the program each year, most of them students of color, and had a wonderful time with them. We created the curriculum together, studied issues of social justice as they applied to the classroom, and experimented with specific ways of teaching and learning through the arts, music, dance, and literature. The program ended bitterly in the fourth year when the university cut it after the funding I had raised ran out. I had put an enormous energy into developing and teaching in the program and during my last year there felt worn down physically and emotionally, not from the teaching, but from constant harassment by the administration.

During the last year of the program, I took to walking randomly around the neighborhoods near the university: wandering into stores, listening to conversations in restaurants, seeking some new focus or adventure, looking for something to seize my heart and inspire me.

I gravitated toward Clement Street, a predominantly Chinese commercial street in western San Francisco. The Clement neighborhood is home to working- and middle-class people, mostly Mainland and Taiwanese Chinese and Koreans with a mix of Asian Americans and a small number of white people who are moving in as the neighborhood begins to gentrify.

Clement is not a tourist destination, but a vibrant community with Chinese, Japanese, and Korean restaurants; vegetable, fish, poultry, and meat markets; pastry shops; teahouses; kitchenware and hardware stores; and the occasional Middle East market. There are a number of tea and coffee bars where older Chinese men play cards, dominoes, and Chinese chess throughout the day. There's even an Irish pub, a wonderful new- and used-book store, and several rock clubs, as well as the usual commerce of an American street: cell phone and computer stores and small markets (*marquetas*) that sell everything from newspapers and candy to cans of soup and lottery tickets.

I struck up a casual friendship with the owner of one of the *marquetas* I frequented. During one of our brief conversations, a policeman came into the store, looked around, and left. As soon as he was out of sight, the owner said that the cop wasn't "real Chinese." I asked him what was "real Chinese," and he said with pride that it was someone who had come from the Mainland. The others in the neighborhood were just Taiwanese. So much for my image of a peaceful diverse community; old scars had been transported across the Pacific.

I had developed the habit of going to lunch one day at Taiwan Restaurant, and then the next day I went to a restaurant diagonally across the street called China First. I didn't really understand until this conversation that every other day I crossed the Strait of Formosa from China to Taiwan and back.

I loved being a stranger on Clement.

On one of my random walks, I encountered a storefront with the sign JOSEPH FINE ARTS SCHOOL. There was a poster in the window that stated that classes in painting, drawing, calligraphy, and sculpture were available. Also on display were samples of students' work and small Chinese sculptured stone figures and painted glass bottles that were for sale. I wondered who Joseph Fine was and decided to go in and look around. For years, I had played around with painting when I was bored, in need of some physical form of meditation. My work was a combination of action painting, abstract expressionism, finger painting—all with no training, grace, or talent. Stumbling upon that school on Clement reminded me of the times I'd promised myself to take painting lessons one day. I decided to enroll in a class whatever the school was like and turn casual painting into an integral part of my new life. It would also bind me in a specific way to the Clement world I was beginning to create as a way of providing some transition to my indefinite future. And it was a way to jump into an arena where I could once more encounter the freshness and excitement of learning things I knew nothing about. It would be new, not a renewal, a childlike pleasure. My current journey's goal was not to regain energy to enter the same old frustrating struggles with renewed energy, but to find a new way to grow and be useful without bringing along the old baggage. I was beginning to admit to myself that many of my theories about educating children were neither relevant nor effective anymore.

I walked into the studio and asked to talk to Joseph Fine. A charming, soft-spoken Chinese couple in their mid-forties came out of the back room to talk to me. They were laughing—there was no Joseph Fine, it was the **Joseph** *Fine Arts School,* and the man introduced himself as Joseph Yan. The studio and school were run by him and his wife, Janny. They said they would be honored to have me as a student.

> *There was a child went forth every day,*
> *And the first object he look'd upon, that object he became,*
> *And that object became part of him for the day, or a certain part*
>   *of the day,*
> *Or for many years, or stretching cycles of years.*
> —WALT WHITMAN, *Leaves of Grass*

The Joseph Fine Arts School is located in a storefront squeezed between a small Chinese market and a Vietnamese restaurant. It runs from Clement Street all the way through to a backyard sculpture garden and fountain. The front room is for sales of art supplies and some imported Chinese art. There are three other rooms along an open corridor leading to the small sculpture garden at the back. The second room is for intermediate and advanced calligraphy and advanced painting. It is also serves as Janny's working place. The third room is for sketching and beginning painting. The last room is for sculpture and other forms of clay modeling. Altogether, about 120 students attend the school during a week.

In the two painting rooms there are tables, some long and some short. At each of the tables there are painting positions set up. A painting station consists of an easel pushed toward the back of the table, an armature to hold brushes, a folded napkin, several plates and small saucers for mixing colors and for ink, and a large rectangular piece of flannel placed on the table.

There were no students present when I wandered into the school, and the setup of the painting positions puzzled me. The easel was pushed so far away from the chair that it would be difficult to reach. And the flannel and tidily folded napkin made no sense to me. I was intrigued and decided that this might be the new and challenging place I was seeking at this stage in my life.

The small ceramic and sculpture studio at the back, leading to an elaborate concrete fountain sculpted and designed by Joseph, also has a kiln and several small potting wheels.

In the inner painting room is a corner set up for pencil drawing. There is a stand for an object, a lamp to light it, and a small easel.

There are Chinese paintings on all of the walls throughout the school. Most of them are Joseph's and Janny's, though some are the works of present and past students.

The entire place is a miracle of packaging. There is no wasted space, yet at the same time it doesn't feel crowded. It was clear to me that someone with a sophisticated spatial sense had designed the school. The source of that aesthetic and spatial intelligence turned out to be Joseph and Janny. They transformed an empty storefront into an elegant, gracious learning environment that projected order, calm, serious work, and playfulness. Usually I enter new places cautiously and with a healthy dose of skepticism probably born out of some of my experiences growing up in the Bronx. But here I immediately felt at home—there was a fairy-tale feeling about my entering Joseph and Janny's world, as if they were waiting for me to take my place in the story. Of course, they weren't, and I wonder what they felt about this older white man walking into their school.

I am certainly not an expert on Chinese painting, but I have been intrigued by it for years. I have looked at Chinese paintings in museums without knowing anything about their history, their relation to one another, the provinces they were painted in, their historical contexts, and/or styles, techniques, and genres. I am literate about much of Western and modern painting and sculpture and feel familiar with their history and character. My tastes are rather broad, and I love seeing one style morph into another over time and to see individual artists transform the traditions they inherit through their own genius. But I knew none of this about Chinese painting. When I entered Joseph's, I could not name one Chinese painter, could not articulate any variations in style or period in the paintings I had viewed in museums and art books, or speculate on the deeper content of the works I saw. Because I couldn't read the poems that are calligraphed directly onto the paintings and whose content is integral to the meaning of the work, many dimensions of the art were inaccessible to me. My knowledge was episodic, and the pleasure I took from the paintings had as much to do with my fantasies about what they meant as with what was actually on the silk or rice paper surfaces. To me they were decontextualized, authorless, generic works much like the African and Oceanic art I still enjoy looking at in museums.

The most puzzling and moving thing to me about Chinese landscape painting was the scale of nature to human life. The people are so small, so modestly placed in overwhelming natural environments, that the latter seem to have more life in them than the people. And the proportion and light are so different from those in Western painting. The air is so clear, the light so diffuse, and the sense of distance so molded by color that perspective and viewpoint, as I understood them in Western painting, are confounded. This is all my personal impression, of course. There is Chinese portrait painting, paintings of birds and flowers and trees, festive and ceremonial people-centered work, and so on. Chinese painting is every bit as varied and complex as Western art, but for me Chinese painting had always meant landscape painting. However, I didn't think much about Chinese paintings when I wasn't passing through a room of them at a museum or skimming through an art book. So when I decided to take lessons at Joseph's, it wasn't particularly for the sake of learning Chinese painting, but for some compelling need I felt to learn in Joseph and Janny's school. My intuition told me to take them on as teachers. Being a student at their school might satisfy my need to escape from everyday worries about my program and metaphysical worries about aging. It would certainly provide a new adventure, which was just what I longed for.

During hard times, I often feel the compelling need for new

growth. For me, learning has always been a form of healing as well as an incentive to growth. To accomplish this, I have always sought new teachers to help me learn in different ways, since the old ways have obviously stopped working. Choosing the right teacher is as important as choosing the right therapist or minister. Joseph and Janny seemed right as teachers, though I had no specific reason to believe it. It was simply a matter of intuition. I like to take chances, and in this case, I had nothing to lose. Their school was so disorienting and attractive that I signed up right away. However, I stayed away from taking a class in Chinese painting—it was just too far out of my experience, and I was afraid to embrace it without some preparation. So I took the conservative path and chose to take pencil drawing for a semester.

For my first drawing lesson, Joseph set up and lit a vase and asked me to draw it. As simple as that. No formal lesson, no manual of technique, no preliminaries. I sat staring at the vase, semiparalyzed, not having the slightest idea how to begin. I sat without putting a mark on my paper.

After a while, Joseph noticed me, came over, and simply said, "I'll show you how to begin." He picked up a pencil and drew the outline of one side of the vase and told me to look at the way it was shaded and to begin shading it. His manner was so encouraging and supportive that I reached out and began drawing. I improved quite a lot and relaxed under Joseph's gentle tutelage. My line became a bit more graceful, and my drawings began to take on volume and weight. The objects I drew became more complex as the semester went on, and it was clear that I was making progress. But I was bored with drawing. Painting was more exciting and seductive. It was the landscapes that attracted me most because they echoed the beauty of the landscapes I live within in Point Arena. At the end of the semester, I decided to ask Joseph if I could take a beginning landscape painting class. He said yes.

My study in Point Arena, California, is surrounded by redwood trees and rock roses, a South African plant that is deer resistant and requires no care other than a few friendly words and a little clipping every few years. I planted the rock roses about twenty years ago. There were two of them about ten inches high, each of which could fit into a medium-size flowerpot. Now they are about four and a half feet high, and the two plants, having run together, create a bush about fifteen feet long. Behind the study is a pond with goldfish and some bottom-feeders. The pond is surrounded by redwoods, fir, alders, pines, madrone, ferns, bracken, and wild shrubs and bushes. I have lived within that landscape since 1977, though I have never painted, filmed, or photographed it. And, sadly, Judy and I have hardly had any time to live at home for about fifteen years, commuting as we have to New York first and then, at the time I began my lessons, to San Francisco.

For a Bronx boy, it's been strange living in the country for over twenty-five years, surrounded by redwoods, a few miles from dairy farms and wild and beautiful beaches. The nearest town has a population of under five hundred. Perhaps there was some subliminal thought, when I decided upon learning to do Chinese landscapes, to painting my way home.

When I showed up for my first lesson, Joseph indicated that I would be in the beginners' class and gave me the tools needed for this new adventure—four animal-hair bamboo brushes, two small, one medium, and one large; rice paper; a bottle of Chinese black ink; and a box of Chinese watercolors, which are made of minerals and organic pigments and don't represent the same color spectrum of Western paintings. There are more earth colors, browns, reds, and vermilions, a yellow, three blues, and white, and one green. Each color has its particular application, and I have still not used them all.

I realized at this ceremonial moment that I would be giving up thoughts of oils and canvas. I would not be working directly from nature, like Cézanne, van Gogh, Poussin, and Turner. Instead I would be giving myself to something thoroughly unknown to me—painting Chinese. Having accepted Joseph as a teacher, I was thus obligated to be a willing and voluntary student, to follow wherever he guided me.

After paying for the brushes and other tools for painting, I followed Joseph to the back painting room, where he settled me at a painting station. I unwrapped my brushes and set them in an armature to my right. Then I opened the box of paints and put them on my left with the bottle of ink. Joseph told me to unroll one sheet of rice paper and place it on the flannel that was in front of me on the table. The flannel would absorb any paint or water that bled through the paper. Then Joseph brought me two coffee cups half filled with water and a folded paper napkin and placed them near the brushes. The easel remained empty, and for the first time I realized that the easel was not for painting. I would be working on the flat surface of the table, painting downward rather than in an upright position as I was accustomed to do when I dabbled with painting at home.

This prepainting ritual—unwrapping the brushes, setting up the painting station, getting water, folding a napkin, placing paper on the flannel mat, and preparing to paint—has become second nature to me. I find it calming, a moment when I move from the pressure of the day to the serene and complex world of Chinese landscape painting.

For that first class, I anticipated meeting a number of Chinese people who could teach me how to play Chinese chess (I love games from all over the world) and introduce me to some aspects of Chinese culture in San Francisco that I had no access to. I took the seat Joseph assigned to me. He had carefully thought out the seating arrangement. There were six painting places and six students (some of my subsequent classes were smaller). There were two desks to my left and three across from me at another table that faced toward the sculpture studio.

The other students began to arrive. The first two went right to their places and prepared to work. The other three, who were first-time students like me, waited for Joseph to help them.

The students were all Chinese or Chinese American. Two of them were five years old, two seven, and one six. Four of them were girls. In terms of skill, I was placed in the right class, but it was a shock. When Joseph said "beginning," he meant it. Education is not age specific for him. Two of the children had taken a prior beginners' class, and they were familiar with the rituals and routines of the work. The experienced painters took out their set of brushes and put them into the armature. They opened their boxes of colors and placed them on the table alongside their bottle of ink; each went to the sink and got two cups of water, and then carefully unrolled a sheet of rice paper and placed it on the felt mat, holding down the corners with wooden blocks just as Joseph had shown me.

Once their places were set, the two more experienced students went to a series of cabinets, picked out paintings to copy, and placed them on their easels. There were dozens of these open cabinets throughout the school that contained rows of paintings mounted on cardboard, numbering perhaps in the hundreds, for use as models for student painting. The easels were to hold paintings to be copied, something I had not expected at all. My whole experience with painting was derived from the notion that you painted directly from nature or life or from your imagination. Copying was considered beneath most young artists I knew. And I would never use it in my teaching because I thought it would inhibit my students' creativity.

Nevertheless, sitting among the children thrilled me. I was a child in school again, this time on my own terms. It's funny how sometimes mind, body, and feelings don't match. I was a child in an old guy's body, and when I sat down that day, my body disappeared and the child in me emerged once again. It was like going home when I had no real childhood home to go back to: parents dead, the Bronx three thousand miles and I can't count how many cultures away. Here I was in a Chinese environment with children I knew nothing about and calm and rested, curious and apprehensive, but delighted. I was on the ground again, a sixty-nine-year-old six-year-old. What fun!

For me, learning is an adventure. It's my way of voyaging, and it requires new settings, new people, and a delicate openness on the part of people you choose to learn from and the students you learn with.

Sitting at my painting station and waiting for Joseph to tell me what to do brought back memories of my own early school days. I remembered my third-grade desk at P.S. 104 on Shakespeare Avenue in the Bronx. I could see the initials carved into it and the inkwell that I had to fill carefully every day. There was my nib pen and the stains that always ended up on my shirts and pants and drove my grandmother crazy.

I hated that class and used to sit in my seat scratching my wrists nervously when I wasn't hiding behind my textbook waiting not to be called on. I could never hold the pen right. The nib split, or I put too much ink on it. My hands were dirty with ink, and I made a complete mess of the assignment and even smeared my textbooks. Still, I loved the idea of writing but was petrified of writing in class. The teacher, Mrs. Katz, showed everyone my papers and made it known that they were too messy for her to bother even reading what I wrote. Eventually, she told my parents, and my father gave me some harsh and unambiguous lessons on how to use a pen and ink.

All of this passed through my mind as I sat at my painting station waiting for Joseph to tell me how to begin. I didn't have the slightest idea of what was about to happen but trusted that the adventure, under Joseph's guidance, would help me voyage into myself and develop a more complex sense of what it means to be older and to embrace the time left for me to be a creative and energetic person in new and unexpected ways.

Joseph chose paintings for me and the other two new students, and I refocused and looked at the scene he chose for me to paint. The Joseph Fine Arts School was not the third grade in the Bronx, and I was not a child and didn't particularly want to be one again. But it was thrilling to be learning among and with children and to be almost on their skill level. The situation reminded me of when I was sent my first computer by Atari (I was on the board of the Atari Foundation, and it was a perk). I couldn't bring myself to open it up because I was so ignorant of the specifics of computing. One day when I came home from work, my children, all under nine at the time, had opened the boxes and were playing games. They had no trouble whatever mastering the system, and over the next few weeks I could play with them and even use the word processor. I have loved learning from children and never been afraid, as many adults seem to be, of showing my lack of knowledge to young people. They love being teachers, and I am a willing student.

The paintings Joseph chose were simple, traditional paintings of monkeys—monkeys playing, eating fruit, swinging on tree limbs, resting, running. There were monkeys by themselves and monkeys in groups. All of them were rendered simply, though there were variations in the inking and coloring. Though each new student was given monkeys to paint, each of us had a different monkey painting to work from. We could copy the classics, but not from one another. It was intriguing—the method for each student was the same, but the content was different. I took out the writing and teaching notebook I always carry and quickly noted that I should try something like the monkey painting in one of my classes at the university.

Nevertheless, I was very self-conscious. I had to focus on my monkeys and not on my self-doubts or the children sitting next to me. I was more than sixty years older than my classmates and had spent over forty years teaching. In the past, I had taught kindergarten and first grade and was proud of my ability to help even the most reticent pupils learn how to read intelligently and write imaginatively. Guiding young people through their encounters with new ideas, skills, and understanding was, and still is, one of the greatest pleasures I know. I wanted to help Joseph's students, provide advice and resources, and be looked up to by them as a caring expert and mentor. Among children I had developed the habit of being a teacher, engaged in their lives and learning. But here Joseph was the teacher, and it quickly became clear that any advice from me, as a novice and a stranger with no structured relation with the children, was inappropriate. Besides, I knew nothing about painting Chinese and couldn't have provided good advice even if it had been asked for. Painting with the children would clearly be a challenge—how to learn painting and accept the awkward position of being simply a student, but one who clearly stood out in the class. What did the children think of my being there? And in some ways even more important, what did their parents think of my being in the class with their children?

It occurred to me that the parents might be worried about my intentions. The issue never came up, though Joseph seemed reassured when I told him I was director of the Center for Teaching Excellence and Social Justice at the University of San Francisco. The parents trusted Joseph and Janny and had confidence that they would not do anything against the interests of their children. There was a bond between the teachers and the parents that had has fundamentally to do with painting on a flat surface and not on an easel. The pinky and the ring finger control the brush near the bristles, though the pinky is rarely used. The thumb and the other two fingers control the top of the brush. The brush is held perpendicular to the surface of the rice paper, as shown in figure 1.

In addition to getting the grip right, Joseph informed me that the brush should be held vertically, as shown in figure 2.

He then asked me to study the monkey while he soaked the brushes in water to dissolve the glue that held the hairs together before use. All of these preliminaries may seem tedious, but holding the brush correctly and caring for the brushes are central to the whole process of Chinese painting, where the tool and the product are integral parts of the activity. They express respect for the art form and acknowledge the importance of tradition in contemporary work.

Attention to ritual slows you down. Often I came to class after a day full of pressure and conflict, of juggling a dozen things at a time, and feeling overwhelmed. Before beginning to paint at Joseph's, I brought all of the complexities of work home to Judy. Now, as soon as I entered the storefront for my lesson, they all temporarily disappeared and the rituals took over. They were my transition from one way of pacing life to another.

As I waited for the glue on my brushes to dissolve, Joseph moved on to the other new students. Once all our brushes were soaked and the brushes softened, Joseph came back to me. I asked him to take care of the children first, but he refused, he said, out of respect for my age and to teach the other students the patience required to do Chinese painting. It was the Chinese way,

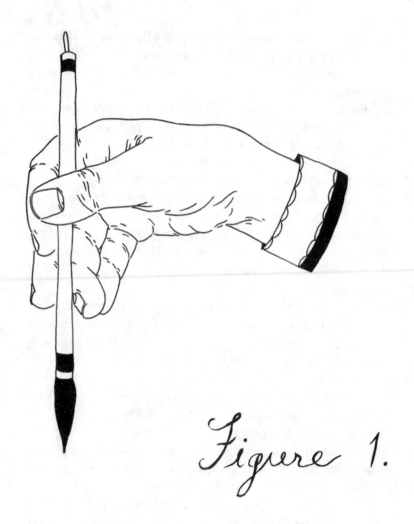

Figure 1.

he explained as he poured a little bit of ink on a saucer and put a daub of red paint on the color-mixing pallet at my place.

My painting portrayed a single monkey holding a red peach. The monkey had a red face. The rest of it was outlined in black, though the body was rendered in shades of gray.

Joseph painted the top of the monkey's head and then gave me the brush, told me to continue the painting, and went to the young girl sitting on my left. Fen couldn't have been more than five years old. She was slim and incredibly well dressed—at least compared with the college students I spent my days working with. She was smiling nervously up at Joseph, and her feet were shaking from anticipation or perhaps anxiety. Joseph spoke to her in the same quiet, reassuring tone that he used with me. And he went through the rituals and details in exactly the same way he did with me. We were both students, novices, and he treated us with the same respect and kindness that I have seen him display toward all the students at the school.

Before beginning to paint, Fen looked closely at her two monkeys. I noticed that Joseph was giving the other students more complex paintings than the one he gave me. He assumed, quite correctly, that I would be the student who had the most trouble with the brush and the rhythm and style of Chinese ink painting.

One of Fen's monkeys was chasing the other, and they both looked somewhat maniacal to me. I noticed her giggle at their antics, as did Joseph. Then he took a medium brush and drew the outline of one of the monkeys' heads and told her to continue. There was no pressure involved; he simply set her out on the road, like a parent giving a gentle push to a child who is learning to ride a bicycle.

The other student on our side of the table, Hui Ying, was very intense. She came into the class and immediately raised her hand. She told Joseph she wanted to be first—first to get her monkeys and first to be taught. He smiled, told her to study the monkeys, and went about his business, paying no attention to her anxious demands. When he finally reached her, she had calmed down a bit. The painting on her easel was of three monkeys sitting in a circle. Joseph got her started on the largest of the three. He also looked over to me and indicated I should look to my painting instead of watching him and the children. Clearly I had to get in painting mode and put aside my desire, as a teacher, to see how the children set about working.

I proceeded with my painting cautiously, dipping my brush first in water and then in ink, though I cheated by watching how Fen worked. Instead of teaching her, I was trying to learn from her. I was afraid to make a mistake, but she showed no such fear and was clearly much more confident than I was. She dipped her brush in the water and then dipped the point into the black ink. Joseph had warned us about getting too much water on the brush. He advised us to ink only the brush's point. I worried about what "too much" meant and just how far the point extended down the brush. I was paralyzed, overly analytic, afraid to make a first stroke. The rice paper was so delicate, and I couldn't figure out any way to erase or correct my mistakes.

I did put too much water and ink on the brush, and as Fen's monkey began to emerge, I made my first watery stroke, watching the ink spread out from my line and create a misty aura around what was to be the top of the monkey's head. I wanted to erase the line, but that was impossible without destroying the sensitive rice paper. My other thought was to tear up the paper and try another one, but before I could get around to it, Joseph came up to me and gently took the brush out of my hand.

I was shocked and embarrassed. Was he telling me that I wasn't capable, that I wasn't ready? I tensed up while he dried off the brush and showed me, slowly, how to do the stroke for the monkey's head by doing it himself. He then inked the brush for me and handed it back without making any judgment, smiled, and encouraged me to go on with the monkey. Later, he added, we could make my stroke into a tree or rock or bamboo. I had just made a stroke, not a mistake. There were no mistakes, just efforts, and, as I later learned, no torn-up papers or restarts in his way of teaching. You just work through what you did no matter what it looks like and use it to teach yourself how to get closer to what you want to achieve in the painting.

Still, I glimpsed Fen's painting with admiration. It was an adorable monkey. She was about to finish up the red around the eyes, nose, and mouth, and I was just beginning to outline the face. She smiled at me and said what I was doing was nice. I didn't agree, but her comment was genuine and supportive. I assume she meant that it was nice that I was trying to paint, and she was right.

Then she turned to her monkey and smiled. She waited for Joseph, who came over and showed her how to dilute the black ink to make a gray to shade its body.

My second attempt was better, and I managed to outline the monkey's head and finish the face in red, though I felt very tense while making my strokes. I noticed how Joseph's strokes flowed and how Fen seemed to paint effortlessly. Their hands, eyes, and minds worked together, while I was worrying about the ink and water, afraid of holding the brush incorrectly, unsure of what pressure to use while making the stroke.

Hui Ying also seemed to be struggling, and I wanted to help her. Joseph sensed my intent and told me, in his quiet voice, that she'd be fine. I checked my impulse to teach and realized that I wouldn't even know how to help her since I was struggling myself. My position was similar to that of experienced teachers who are required to teach subject matter they do not know. The desire to help students is there, the skill and craft of supporting and encouraging students is there, the ability to motivate and help others through new challenges is there. But the substance, the content, the subject matter itself, is a barrier to effective teaching. Trying to teach what you don't yet know is a compromise at best, and even the most talented teachers, when forced into that situation, can at best learn with their students as they work to stay a bit ahead of them. For me at Joseph's, helping the other students was not a possibility. I was truly headed into unknown territory, and it was clear over the course of the semester that the other students, having seen brothers and sisters and friends learn Chinese painting, were better prepared for the experience than I was.

The third new student, Chen, was the youngest of us. He worked quickly and produced a delightful monkey who was throwing a peach. I couldn't see how he worked; he was across the table, hidden by his easel. However, every few minutes he would get up and walk around, looking at everything else that was going on in the room. Joseph had to stare him back to work but was very

patient with him. Joseph acted with confidence and trust. He knew everyone would settle into painting and gave us the space and support to do it in our own ways. There was no disorder in the room at all; rather, there was a gentle, almost imperceptible, hum of people doing joyful work.

The other two students, the old-timers, painted confidently. Lynn, the oldest of the children, was serious about her work. I noticed Joseph spent time teaching her more complex techniques than the rest of us were ready for. His technique was simply to demonstrate, on a separate piece of paper or on a napkin, a stroke or way of mixing paints. He did it once and then let her figure out how to integrate it into her work. The fifth child, Pearl, was very playful and voluble. At times, she couldn't resist chatting with other students, but Joseph managed to refocus her whenever she lost concentration and began to socialize. It was clear that Joseph's priority was to nurture our artistic expression.

I already felt like a bad student. I hadn't given myself a chance, but I was pushing too hard, perhaps because of the awkwardness of painting with the children. I didn't know how to be just another student, alongside them. I was one of them as a student, but I certainly wasn't an elementary school child. Usually I am relaxed and willing to take chances when facing a new challenge. Competition doesn't interest me. In my teaching, I'm relaxed with my students and encourage them to push themselves without worrying about competition or the possibility of failure. Yet there I was doing and feeling everything I discouraged in my students.

I even tied my anxiety to age. Maybe I was too old to learn something completely new. For an instant, I thought of giving up.

Fortunately, Joseph came over to me during this moment of self-indulgent negativity and said that my monkey's face looked good. I immediately felt that he was putting me on and then checked myself and took another look at the monkey. I had never done anything like this before, and for a first effort I had to admit it wasn't too bad. And in retrospect, I understand that most of this anxiety was imported from the conflicts I was having at the university and had nothing directly to do with the painting or my fellow students.

On reflection, I know I was overanalyzing and overreacting to the whole situation, but there was no doubt that there was some personal metaphysical crisis underlying my engagement with the Joseph Fine Arts School. And this was only the first lesson.

After a few weeks, I came simply to enjoy painting with the children and left my anxieties at my office. The children's work was charming, and they managed to capture the wicked spirit of the monkeys. They were thinking about the monkeys, not the painting. I was thinking about the painting and not enough about the monkeys.

However, it became clear to me that I could stumble my way through class without worrying about being judged inadequate. As I became comfortable in this new setting, after a few weeks that wicked spirit appeared in my work, too. I still struggled with the brush, but it didn't bother me as much anymore. There was time for mastery and no one rushing me toward goals or objectives. There were no tests, no schedules. All the external threats that often inhibit learning were not there. I was learning to paint Chinese in a supportive and pleasant environment, and that was it.

There were moments of friction, however. Hui Ying still waved her hand wildly when she wanted Joseph's attention and took to looking at my painting before class and giving me advice about the right way to hold the brush or organize my tools on the table or place my rice paper on the felt mat. I became her project for a few weeks and tried to integrate her suggestions into my rituals and work. I tried to orient myself to being taught by a child, especially one I didn't particularly like. I'm not sure why I listened to her, even though there were times her advice was helpful and I certainly agreed with her critique of my work. I think it may have been something I developed in my years of teaching—listening to my students and trying out their suggestions, sometimes against my better judgment. I tried always to err on the side of the children.

For a while, Joseph observed all of this without saying anything, but one day he came up to me and said, "She's been to regular school too long and learned bad habits. Just paint from your heart."

Indirectly, he let me know that he was the teacher and that I shouldn't let this feisty six-year-old lead me astray, nor should I get frustrated with her. Moreover, he was implying that Chinese children were more respectful and that if she stayed the course at the school, she would learn to relax, to respect her teacher more, and to develop the fine art of patience. She would also develop the capacity to be creative without worrying about competition or approval. She was facing the same learning challenges I was, and in that light I began to think more kindly of her. My irritation had to be tempered by patience, a lack of attachment to performance, and an appreciation of her anxiety.

Unable to fully detach from the teacher in me, I observed Joseph work with Hui Ying while trying to paint. He never came to her on demand, but when it was her turn he gave her a lot of time and instruction. Without a word, she began to relax and give up her competitive ways, at least for the time she was at Joseph's. As my lessons went on and I had a chance to observe the children over time, I could see that they were developing self-discipline, confidence, pleasure in their own achievements, and, most of all, patience with their own learning. Ironically, by abandoning competition in this gentle and encouraging environment, they were acquiring strengths and skills that would serve them well in a competitive learning environment, where self-discipline and focused work are the essence of academic success. It even occurred to me that Joseph's way of teaching, if it was widespread through informal learning experiences in the Chinese community, might partially account for the amazing success of Chinese and Chinese American students in schools.

Before Chaos was divided, Heaven and Earth were one;
All was a shapeless blur, and no men had appeared.
Once Pan Gu destroyed the Enormous Vagueness
The separation of pure and impure began.
Living things have always tended toward humanity;
From their creation all beings improve.

—WU CHENG'EN, *Journey to the West*

One day after class, I overheard Fen telling her mother that the biggest monkey in her painting was Monkey King, and I thought her creation of a story from her painting was ingenious and delightful. The next week, I mentioned this to Joseph, and he laughed and told me all Chinese children knew Monkey King. Curious about Monkey King's identity, I set out to learn more about him. I wanted to know what my fellow students knew and have an understanding of what they brought culturally to the painting of monkeys and to Chinese painting in general. I intuited that there was a complex of cultural knowledge and sensibility that informed Joseph's thinking and the children's experience of painting Chinese, and I wanted to understand it. Maybe I would also learn why Joseph began his curriculum with monkeys. I wasn't aware of the journey it would set me on.

A few blocks from the Joseph Fine Arts School, there is a small book, newspaper, and Chinese painting supply store. The newspapers and magazines are all in Chinese, as are the great majority of the books, though there are some in English about Chinese language, literature, and thought. There is also a section of Chinese painting instruction books, most reprints of classical texts, though some are both recent and bilingual. I enjoyed dropping into the shop and chatting with the owner even before I began my lessons with Joseph and Janny.

When I wanted to find out about the Monkey King, naturally, I went to the shop and asked the owner if he had ever heard of him. There were other people in the shop, and the patron addressed something to them in Mandarin or Cantonese, and they all laughed. Then he said to me, "All Chinese know Monkey King," and beckoned me to follow him to the back of the shop, where he took down a four-volume boxed paperbound set of a 2,317-page-long novel called *Journey to the West*. He told me this was the story of Monkey King. The novel was written during the Ming dynasty by Wu Cheng'en and published in 1592. It is a mythologized version based on the journey of the monk Xuan Zang (602–664), who traveled from China to India to obtain sacred documents of Buddhism and bring them back to China. On his return with the documents, Xuan Zang translated them into Chinese, which according to historians contributed to the growth of Buddhism in China.

I bought the set and discovered the extraordinary journey that begins with the birth of Monkey King, the most amazing superhero I have ever encountered. The Monkey King is a trickster, an Anansi, a Br'er Rabbit, or a Coyote on a cosmic scale, and his tale begins with a rock on top of a mountain:

"There once was a magic stone on the top of this mountain that was thirty-six feet five inches high and twenty-four inches round. It was thirty-six feet and five inches high to correspond with the 365 degrees of the heavens, and twenty-four feet round to match the twenty-four divisions of the solar calendar. On top of it were nine apertures and eight holes, for the Nine Palaces and the Eight Trigrams. There were no trees around it to give it shade, but magic fungus and orchids clung to its side. Ever since Creation began it had been receiving the truth of Heaven, the beauty of Earth, the essence of the Sun and the splendor of the Moon;

and as it had been influenced by them for so long it had miraculous powers. It developed a magic womb, which burst open one day to produce a stone egg about the size of a ball.

"When the wind blew on this egg it turned into a stone monkey, complete with five senses and four limbs. When the stone monkey had learned to crawl and walk, he bowed to each of the four quarters. As his eyes moved, two beams of golden light shot towards the Pole Star palace."

Monkey King has no parents and is of special interest to the Buddha and the Immortals because of his miraculous birth and the power it conveyed to him. He is taken under the wing of one of Buddha's ten major disciples, Subhuti, who gives him the name Sun Wukong. *Sun* means "monkey," and its ideogram contains one element that means "male" and another that means "baby." Sun Wukong has many characteristics of a man but also is selfish, irresponsible, defiant, playful, charming, and above all energetic like a small child. *Wu* means "awakened," and *Kong* means "emptiness." The whole name means "monkey awakened to false emptiness." As the text says about the name: "When the great Vagueness was separated there were no Surnames; To smash foolish emptiness he [Sun Wukong] had to be awakened to emptiness."

Foolish emptiness is concern for the empty rewards of the world, for riches and power, for appearances rather than spiritual reality, which in Buddhist thinking is a form of true emptiness and receptivity. Monkey King needs to be awakened to emptiness in order to journey toward Buddhahood. Awakened emptiness is, according to the author of the novel, on the Positive side, and Sun

Wukong's journey was from the Negativeness ascendant in him at the time of his strange birth to the Positive side. And a long journey it was.

The whole concept of the Positive side and the Taoist opposition between positive and negative intrigued me. They are not the same as good and evil, and emptiness does not involve confession and absolution so much as developing a higher level of consciousness, a journey toward a fuller understanding of what's important in life. In a way, I was seeking true emptiness, a removal from unnecessary struggles, anxieties, and fears, and that's what drove me to seek out Joseph.

I imagined I was accompanying Monkey King on his journey while painting monkeys and watching the children paint monkeys. I was aware that the children and Joseph knew more about monkeys than I did, and the mystery of their knowledge intrigued and challenged me.

In the beginning, Sun Wukong was on the Negative side and a hopeless apprentice to the Immortal Subhuti, fighting demons but leaving disaster in his wake. He uses magical powers he obtains from Subhuti to satisfy his ego and its worldly ambitions. He even tries to storm Heaven and achieve immortality.

Monkey King has the ability to ride clouds at close to the speed of light and the ability to tear out his own hairs and turn them into an army of monkey clones that fight alongside him. He has also obtained a magical gold-ringed staff that can be reduced and expanded to any length and given any strength. He miniaturizes it and keeps it hidden behind his earlobe, where he can draw it out and transform it at will. The most common visual representations of Sun Wukong are of a monkey in warrior's dress with a small crown on his head and his fighting stick enlarged and at the ready. In many of them, he is also riding on a cloud.

Monkey King's defiance of authority and capacity to stir up trouble are well-known throughout China. During the Cultural Revolution, Mao Zedong proclaimed, "The local areas must produce several more Sun Wukongs to vigorously create a disturbance at the Palace of Heaven."

In an ironic departure from Mao, I also recently discovered that Sun Wukong is on the short list to be the mascot of the 2008 Olympics in Beijing.

During one of my lessons, I asked Joseph if that first monkey I was painting, the one with a red peach, was Sun Wukong. I had learned that Sun Wukong was appointed guardian of the Sacred Peaches of Immortality, a job he failed in by eating peaches and achieving immortality without achieving enlightenment. Joseph just chuckled and made a suggestion about the painting I was working on. He left it to me to figure out, a strategy consistent with what I began to feel was a part of his Buddhist-influenced philosophy.

The children painted monkeys with gusto and swept me along with them. They laughed at their monkeys, loved looking at them, and ran to their parents after class to show off their paintings. After three or four weeks of painting monkeys, I also began to show off my work to Judy and my children, who were delighted, as much with seeing me relaxed and happy as with the work itself. During the first two months, including practice time at home, I continued to learn how to think less about how to hold and ink the brush and more about monkeys. Toward the end of the time we were painting monkeys, the scenes we copied got more and more complex. One of the last monkey paintings I did in class was of a band of monkeys eating peaches.

As a punishment for eating the peaches and in despair of ever controlling Sun Wukong, he was buried in a furnace under a mountain, where he was left to burn for centuries. Being made of stone, the furnace didn't affect Monkey King, but the heat and intense fire turned his eyes to golden crystal that could look through things and see things other people couldn't. Throughout his adventures, Monkey King starts out badly, gets punished, and then turns the punishment to his benefit. As he says later in *Journey to the West* when some of his traveling companions worry about him: "This has always been my way of doing business: I lose out at first and win in the end."

This reminds me of the motto I have tried, not always successfully, to use to guide my own work as an educator: *Festina lente*, make haste slowly.

For all Monkey King's troublemaking, Buddha understands that Monkey King's mischief is just part of his journey to enlightenment. Ultimately, Sun Wukong is chosen to accompany the monk and holy man Tripitaka on a journey to India in the West to obtain the holy books of Buddhism and return them to China in order to spread the teachings of Buddhism among the people.

Monkey King could not be fully trusted to act appropriately on the journey, so he was fitted with a gold headband that would tighten when Tripitaka thought it was necessary. It was to be used only in extreme situations of danger. One of the challenges for the Monkey King was to remain himself while becoming enlightened and internalizing the teachings of the Buddha. The road to enlightenment in Buddhism, and in my life, never comes without some pain and suffering.

While I was reading the novel, it occurred to me that the headband acted as a conscience or a superego that was initially imposed and finally absorbed into the Monkey King's being. I know that when I'm troubled, I feel it in my head. It's as if something internal is pulling at me and telling me that I'm heading toward trouble or being tempted to act against my conscience. I have to admit to identifying with Sun Wukong. His journey has gotten me thinking about my own journey to the West. I was born in a working-class community in the Bronx in 1937, went to New York City public schools, and in 1954 went to Harvard. After graduation in 1958, I traveled east to Europe for a year and returned to work in the New York City public schools. My wife, our six-month-old daughter, and I began our journey to the West at Christmastime 1967 when we moved to Berkeley. We moved to rural Point Arena in Mendocino County, California, in 1977, and we still live there for most of the year. However, over the last ten years I've commuted to first New York and then San Francisco, always returning to Point Arena, which is one of the westmost points of California. Unlike the journey Monkey King embarked on, I did not return to the East. I have found treasures in the West, most notably my own children, my students, and the friendships I've developed since coming to California. Unlike Monkey King, I do not have a place to return to. Reading about Monkey King's journey has become a vehicle for thinking about the structure of my own life and the meaning of home in the context of no return. The place where I was born does not exist anymore. The Bronx of 2005 is not the Bronx of 1937, nor can it be, which reminds me of one of the plaints of my father's mother and father. My grandparents were immigrants from Eastern Europe and for years thought about returning home. My grandfather did not even get his citizenship papers until the 1940s, although he arrived on Ellis Island in 1905. He decided to get the papers when he learned that his village had been obliterated by the Nazis. There was no home for him to go to, a wound he never recovered from. As I get older, I find myself thinking and dreaming more about the Bronx of my childhood than I have in the past. Someday I hope to paint the feeling of this longing in the style of a Chinese landscape with this poem by Li Po as the accompanying inscription:

THE POET THINKS OF HIS OLD HOME
I have not turned my steps toward the East Mountain for so long.
I wonder how many times the roses have bloomed there . . .
The white clouds gather and scatter like friends.
Who has a house there now to view the setting of the bright moon?

One of the aspects of being older I find most moving is the ability to think of one's life as a voyage. Painting Chinese has led me to focus on that journey in a way that has begun to help me understand the shape of my life. Each painting is a journey for me, a transformation of an empty page into a world of my creation that helps me think about my current life and feelings. Some of my friends have joked that reading Monkey King and painting with the children are just multicultural adventures for me. But that's not how I see it. Though *Journey to the West* and Sun Wukong are Chinese, and though I am painting Chinese with Chinese and Chinese American children, my engagement is personal. I hope to enrich my store of metaphors and images, develop new skills of meditation and concentration, and learn more about my place in the world at this time in my life. I too want to journey toward awakened emptiness and be, like Monkey King, on the side of the Positive during these Negative days. And I constantly remind myself, sitting among the children in class, that they or their families have also made journeys to the East across the Pacific to a land with a different language and culture. I watch them living between two cultures, trying to preserve Chinese culture and tradition while becoming thoroughly American.

The children all go to English-language schools and speak English fluently. Most of them also speak Mandarin with ease. Some of their parents don't speak much English at all. In the safe haven of the Joseph Fine Arts School, they can be their complex selves, speaking any language they choose, relating to Chinese painting and sculpture after spending most of their day in American schools. It would be wonderful if monolingual, monocultural Anglos could understand and embrace the idea of complex intercultural and cross-cultural lives. At the school, in a modest way supported by reading, research, and developing acquaintanceships within the Chinese community, I feel that is what I am doing.

Monkey King's journey was long and complex, providing a cornucopia of images and metaphors to provoke thinking about growth and the challenges of aging. The journey has nine times nine, or eighty-one, trials. Nine is a magical number in Chinese thinking and is on the Positive side. In the *I Ching*, the number 9 represents a crucial point of change and transition.

I won't recount the delightful, often wise tales that accompany each of the trials, but I found the eighty-first and final trial, before the scriptures were finally delivered to China, of particular significance for understanding the whole text and—more significant for me personally—for understanding a bit more about what I might encounter on my journey through the last decade or two of my life.

Sun Wukong and the other voyagers were within six miles of a Chinese village and decided to rest in the mountains for the night before arriving home. That night, there was a wild storm.

Now the wind, mist, thunder, and lightning were all signals made by evil demons who wanted to steal the scriptures. They tried all night to grab them until the dawn; only then did they stop.

The venerable elder, whose clothes were all soaking wet, shivered and shook as he said, "How did this start, Wukong?"

"Master," Brother Monkey replied, snorting with fury, "you don't understand the inner truth. By escorting you to fetch these scriptures, we have won the great achievement of Heaven and Earth . . . the thunder could not bombard them, the lightning could not illuminate them, and the mist could not obscure them. It was also because I whirled my iron cudgel around to make its pure Positive nature protect them. Since the dawn the Positive has been in the ascendant again, which is why they can't take them now."

A little later, when the sun was shining from high in the sky, they took the scriptures to the top of a cliff, opened the bundles, and put them out to dry. The rocks on which the scriptures were dried in the sun remain there to this day."

The next morning the townsfolk, who had heard of their return, prepared a feast, so the voyagers had to pack up the texts they had laid out to dry and wrap them carefully before descending. However, the novel goes on:

"It was not realized that the ends of several rolls of the Buddha-caritakavya sutra had stuck to the rock when wet, and the ends were torn off, which is why the Buddha-caritakavya sutra is incomplete to this day, and there are still traces of writing on the rocks where the scriptures were dried in the sun. Tripitaka said with remorse, 'We did not pay enough attention.'

"'You're wrong,' said Monkey with a laugh, 'you're wrong. Heaven and Earth are incomplete, and this scripture used to be complete. Now it's been soaked and torn to fulfill the mystery of incompleteness. This is not something that could be achieved through human effort.'"

Sun Wukong is no longer the troublemaker, and he speaks in a wise and enlightened voice at the end of the novel. The journey has purified him, and as a reward he becomes a Buddha with the title "Buddha Victorious in Strife." Monkey King has come to the end of his journey, still somewhat wicked but on the side of the Positive. My journey was still in progress, and my painting lessons and lessons for life were just beginning.

In an age of magic, technique is completely identified with the power to make magic. The greatest technician is also the greatest magician. The strength of the spell grows with the ability to paint. . . . [The painter's] artistic skill was only regarded as the measure of his power to make magic.

—FRITZ VAN BRIESSEN, *The Way of the Brush*

I became sidetracked by Monkey King. But Joseph and the lessons moved on past monkey paintings to panda bears and bamboo. I tried my hand at a few panda bears, but they didn't move me at all, and Joseph must have sensed my boredom because he moved me quickly on to the painting of bamboo. I still struggled with the brushes. Sometimes they were under control. At other times they simply would not do what I wanted. Too much water. Too much ink. Too little water, too much ink. Too much ink, too little water. Every permutation and combination possible. The brush would split or leave a wet streak, making what I considered to be a bloody mess. I couldn't keep the point sharp, and my lines became too wide or blurred. I began studying more carefully what the children were doing as they learned how to paint, and I believe Joseph relaxed a bit with my role and was somewhat amused by my participatory research.

I discovered the children had an organic relationship to the brushes while I had a critical relationship to them. I knew what an organic relationship to tools meant from something that happened

when I was about their age. My grandfather was a framer, a rough carpenter who used two-by-fours to frame in walls, windows, and floors. He had a framing hammer that had a long handle and was heavy at the top. The handle was worn from I don't know how many years of use. You could practically see the imprint of his palm and fingers on it. One day I took the hammer out of his toolbox and hid it before my grandfather went to work. He checked his toolbox as he always did before setting off to work and saw that the hammer was gone. I saw a look of panic on his face, as if an old friend had died or abandoned him, and got very scared. I ran and got him the hammer, and, as kind to me as he always was, he said in Yiddish, "If you ever do this again, I'll brain you." He wasn't kidding, and I think since that time I've thought of people's tools as sacred.

For the children the brush was a friend, a familiar, an extension of the hand. For me, initially, it was an object to conquer. When I stopped fighting the brush, I painted well, and when I thought too much about it, my painting became a mess. There is a wise thoughtlessness, a creative freedom, that develops when tool, person, thought, emotion, and activity are one. Young children can be creative and imaginative in ways most adults can't. Overteaching and rigid rules force young children to perform in a rigid way, destroying this organic gift. As an older person, I had to let go to get back to that place that comes so naturally to children.

My situation with the children was awkward. I wanted to talk to them, get to know what they were thinking and not just observe what they were doing. But there were social, cultural, age, and gender boundaries I could not cross. I was a stranger, a grown-up among children, a student, not a researcher or teacher.

Nevertheless, I was determined to understand more about the students—but, more important, get the painting right. Fortunately, there was no right and wrong for Joseph, just working to paint your personal vision of the world and the spirit. Joseph was interested in authentic painting, not "good" painting. I was beginning to understand Buddhist teaching and creative detachment. It was a matter of forgetting about being judged and being fully engaged in your work.

Despite Joseph's occasional admonitions, I watched the children as they painted. Sometimes they worked with ease and grace, though clearly there were times when they experienced the same frustration I did. Fen's work was graceful, and she obviously took to the brush. Her strokes were made with confidence, and her monkeys and pandas had character. She managed to set their mouths in wicked smiles or pouts or smirks; she didn't merely copy the monkeys, but infused them with life. Her pandas were equally expressive and were transformed copies, in many ways true to the composition, color, and shape of the original but with a delightful personal touch that echoed her own charm, humor, and confidence.

I remember she asked Joseph if she had to copy the panda just as it was on the original, and he smiled and said paint it as you feel it, make the panda alive. She understood, and I noticed her strokes got more graceful and her colors became a bit wilder. Her pandas became more expressive, and you felt them as individuals, not just copies of a standard panda.

Fen noticed that I was watching her painting (I avoided looking her straight in the eyes, as it would have been bad manners and possibly misinterpreted). She took to showing me her work after class, and I praised it, not too effusively and not at great length. I was learning from Joseph to act with restraint and to curb my Bronx enthusiasms. I felt it was essential that my responses fit with the cultural mode of the school, which likely derived from some unspoken norms of Chinese culture.

I watched Fen mix with the other children, and it seemed that she got along with everyone, although once there was some friction when she tried to tell Lynn, who was older, what picture to choose from the files for her next painting. Lynn didn't like it, and I anticipated conflict and disruption of what to me was a very serene environment. I had experienced many budding conflicts like this in the kindergarten and first-grade classes I taught and prepared myself to intervene, forgetting that it wasn't my place to do it. However, before I had a chance to do anything, Joseph walked up to the girls and suggested that Fen add some detail to her panda and Lynn begin with the painting he had chosen for her. He didn't say a word about the tension, didn't admonish either of them; he simply refocused them on painting. Like all good teachers, he was attuned to what was happening among his students and knew exactly when to intervene in order to prevent trouble from surfacing. He anticipated the problem and was in a position to defuse it. It is a skill very difficult to teach. In this case I admired the ease, skill, firmness, and above all gentleness with which Joseph managed the situation. Both girls went back to painting, and nothing came of the incident. Fen even nodded toward me, making it clear that she knew she was being observed. I wanted to chat with her about what happened, but Joseph gave me a look that said get back to painting. On reflection, this was wonderful advice, since my goal was to find a new way of doing things and not indulge old habits of teaching. Joseph was helping me refocus, without distraction, on the brush, the paper, the ink, and the image.

Hui Ying was having trouble with the pandas. Her goal was to get the panda exactly right, line by line, color by color, shade by shade. Some of her pandas were delightfully irregular, and she got angry at them but knew that tearing up a painting and starting over again was simply not an option. At one point, I thought she was on the verge of tears. She looked toward me. When Joseph came over to help me, I suggested he go to her first, and he replied that she needed to develop patience with her work, to study it and sit with it for a while. She needed to be ready to be helped, and he was giving her time to think about her work. After a while, she did calm down, and by the time he went over to help her, she was more relaxed and ready to take advice and paint with greater ease and grace.

I certainly identified with what she was going through because my challenge, in painting and in life in general, was to ease up on myself. One of my problems with becoming older was a stubborn refusal to accept the inevitable slowing down that comes with age. I continued to work twelve hours a day, even though occasionally I almost passed out from exhaustion. I took on new projects when I was already overwhelmed with old ones. In the past, I was somehow able to complete things, but increasingly I couldn't keep up with myself. I needed to learn to live and learn and create at a slower pace and with less ambition. I didn't always have to be at the forefront of educational change or close to the center of innovation. And, though I enjoyed my teaching, I began to realize that about three-quarters of the time I functioned in a mechanical way, going through rituals and routines that had come to bore me.

There was nothing mechanical about the children's painting. Chen, for example, wandered about looking at everyone's painting. He had some trouble with the brushes and the ink, but that didn't seem to bother him at all. He admired his work and went quickly from one series of monkeys to another, even if they sometimes bore no resemblance to the originals. Joseph let him move in this high-velocity mode and told me that he would grow into more complex and deliberate painting in time. Joseph was not impatient with his impatience. When Joseph gave me bamboo to paint, Chen asked to paint bamboo, too. I heard him tell Joseph, pointing at me, "I want to paint what that guy is painting." Perhaps he felt we were the two guys in the class and therefore should be doing the same thing. Joseph told Chen that one day he would be painting bamboo, but he wasn't ready yet. He went back to racing through monkeys and pandas and seemed to have forgotten about the bamboo.

Meanwhile, Pearl and Lynn painted with intensity and discipline, and their work was very impressive to me. They had finished the beginning sequence of exercises and had mastered color, the brushes, and the inks on a preliminary level. At that point, Joseph asked them what they wanted to paint. Pearl chose birds, and Lynn chose flowers. A little more than halfway through the semester, the class had diversified. Three students were painting pandas, one bamboo, one birds, and one flowers. We all developed organically, and Joseph moved among us with ease and grace.

Joseph orchestrated the class in a quiet, indirect way. He knew what each student was doing and knew when we experienced uncertainty or frustration. He was aware of our efforts and available to help us and keep us focused on the challenges of the work. We all waited for his attention when we came to a problem. Once when I asked him about this, he told me that for him waiting was a very important skill. It gave the painter time to reflect on the work, to consider what the problem seemed to be, and to come up with a solution even before he came to help. Certainly I found that during these periods of waiting for his attention, I looked more closely at my own work, thought about my brushstrokes, and looked to the children for inspiration and understanding of the process. I also realized that the patience he was imparting would serve the children well in their school careers and in their lives.

The children were also patient with me. Before and after class, we greeted one another; at times they helped me set up my painting space, and I felt comfortable in their presence without having to be in a position where I was teaching them. Our relationship was a combination of formal and casual, but when painting began, we all retreated into our own worlds.

Patience is a much overlooked virtue in our culture. I grew up in an impatient world. I always arrive early to meetings, can't stand waiting for people to show up for appointments, worry about getting things done on time. Joseph was helping me integrate patience and noncritical self-consciousness into my painting and my life. I was beginning to see that the endless voyage of learning to paint Chinese, the unachievable, had a deeper meaning for me. I had to make haste slowly through aging and on to death. There was no need for urgency. Urgency is at the core of my old-age crisis. I feel that there are so many things I want to do, so many books to read, people I would like to know, friends I would like to spend time with, children I would like to teach, and books I want to write. However, I am aware that I need to overcome worrying about that in order to achieve what I can with the time left to me.

Copy the old masters.

—HSIEH HO, *Six Canons of Painting*

I set up a Chinese painting place in my study at our home in the country—felt pad, armature, easel, and all. It was almost like a shrine, and I bought a bamboo plant and placed it next to the easel in a decorated Chinese bamboo vase I bought in the store next door to the school. When we were at home on weekends, I practiced monkeys and later bamboo. It took a while, but my shaky monkeys began to develop energy. At good moments, I forgot about getting the brush and the strokes right and also about copying. I was rendering the copied monkeys in my own way. The original provided me with the structure within which I could express my own sense of the delightful wickedness and mischievousness of monkeys. I was beginning to feel the meaning in the painting— even monkey was becoming more than monkey. Joseph from the very beginning impressed on me the importance of being in your painting and infusing it with meaning and spirit. He said, "Paint from within." There was something more to copying than just copying, and it took me a while to understand what it was.

In class, I reluctantly gave up painting monkeys and went on to bamboo, which I fell in love with. As with the monkeys, I realized that the children knew bamboo in ways I could never understand. Bamboo is ceremonial, decorative, omnipresent in Chinese culture, and children hear stories about it, have it growing in their homes, and in a profound way take it for granted as part of their cultural and physical environment. They are old friends and delightful to paint.

The overlapping leaves of bamboo resemble the Chinese character *an*, which means "peace and security." A popular Chinese saying is, "Bamboo brings tidings of peace." It is a custom of many Chinese families to hang a painting of bamboo in their home to bring peace and well-being to their family. Many of my fellow students certainly knew that.

About the time I started painting bamboo, I gave a talk at a conference on education and mentioned that I was trying to learn Chinese brush painting. After the talk, a woman came up to me and shared that she too had taken lessons in brush painting. She wondered whether I too had to do monkeys, pandas, and bamboo, adding that she got completely bored with the entire copying thing and stopped her lessons. Up to that point, I had assumed, without thinking much about it, that Joseph and Janny had crafted their own curriculum. But that was silly—of course they had traditions to draw on. They too were teaching copying, but in their own way, piecing together from tradition a curriculum appropriate to their current goals as educators and their students' capabilities and motivations.

Copying is held in high esteem in Chinese painting. As Hsieh Ho says in his fifth-century work *Six Canons of Painting*, "On copying, seek to pass on the essence of the masters' brush and methods." It is the search for that essence that makes copying high art. It is a question not of exact reproduction, but of living through the process that the master used to create his work.

Copying in Chinese painting is a route to learning within a tradition in order to eventually place your work within that tradition in a unique and transformed way. Joseph told me that when he went to art school in China, he spent his early years copying but that in the last years of his study, all of his class was assigned to go into the mountains and experience and sketch the nature represented in the masterworks of the traditions. They were learning to relive the inspiration of their ancestors.

Not all Chinese art is so "classical," but the work that Joseph and Janny teach is. In fact, I believe they are inspired partially by the desire to preserve and pass on this tradition in the United States, where it is so easy to disrupt continuity with one's artistic, cultural, and historical past. The children know this, and their parents encourage it. It is a way of preserving identity, as their children, most of whom are academically successful, will internalize their Chinese identity. It is part of their preservation of identity in the adventure that living in California engages them in. And it's also part of my adventure to renew myself as I grow older and lose old skills. It's the newness I need at this stage in my life: my kindergarten as well as the children's.

Still, I was uneasy about copying, given that I'd previously assumed mechanical copying inhibited creativity and was akin to painting by numbers. Recently, I mentioned that I was learning Chinese brush painting to an old and dear friend, the educational philosopher Maxine Greene. She immediately responded that she had been to China not long ago and had the chance to observe children who were learning to paint. She was upset by what she saw. "Copying, that's all they were doing, copying," she said, and went on to claim that the very act was crushing creativity and possibly turning the students into unthinking mechanical adults unprepared for functioning in democratic ways. I've never been to China and certainly don't know how they structure education in the arts. Personally, I found copying an important way to become comfortable with new tools and an unfamiliar aesthetic and spiritual sensibility.

In fact, the other students were often mischievous, deliberately changing or exaggerating expressions, embellishing on the original. They were not inhibited in any way. Fen liked to add a flower or two to her painting, Hui Ying would change the colors of the originals, and Chen would play with every form but within the structure he was given for the overall assignment. And Joseph encouraged such independence within the context of traditional structure.

One day, I asked Joseph about copying, and his simple response was that copying was art and that a good copy of a masterwork is a valuable work of art in itself. A little research revealed to me that copying and imitation are not opposed to creativity in Chinese art, as they are in many progressive Western educational philosophies. In fact, in my own teaching, I have always encouraged students to create their own works and not copy. I separated looking at classical works from creating one's own work, the emphasis being on personal innovation and freedom of expression. I still believe that this open encouragement of children to "express themselves" is valuable and should be a component of art education. But copying—that is, rendering a classical work through one's own perception of it—is also illuminating and enriching. In Chinese painting, it is a way of understanding how the painter saw the world as well as learning about her or his technique. For me, it is a personal exercise that involves empathy, heightened perception, and developing new skills while suspending old habits of perception and beliefs. I was a novice participant as a painter and at the same time an experienced educator struggling to enrich my understanding of how people (myself included) learn. I was also a traveler without a map, trying to determine a path for the last years of my life. The decision to take lessons in painting Chinese has turned out to be a major factor in my thinking about the future, as psychoanalysis was during my confused early twenties before I decided to pursue a childhood dream and become a teacher and writer.

Copying classical Chinese painting is also good preparation for copying from nature. I began to understand this when I was starting to copy landscapes and asked Joseph to loan me some of the paintings he used in his curriculum to work on them at home. He refused and told me to paint from the nature that surrounded me at home in Point Arena. I had told him of the redwoods, of the ocean, of the hills and valleys. My response was that it would be very difficult for me to do non-easel painting from nature without bringing along a table and chair and setting up the equivalent of a miniature studio out in nature, even though the idea did intrigue me. His response was to tell me to sketch first and then bring the sketch and my memories and feelings about the place back to the classical landscapes. Copying from nature is not that much different from copying a master painting from this perspective. You have to study the masterwork and feel your way into it as much as you do in nature. And the reward for me has been the development of quieter, heightened perception and love of the details of rocks, tree, paths, roads, birds, and other facets of a scene. It has also moved me toward a nonreligious spiritual perception of nature and history and my modest place in it. I am not affiliated with a formal religion, though I am in awe of the creation of the stars and the complexity of life in all its forms. The best way I can describe it at this point is that I am reverent but not religious.

When I try to think through the nature of creative copying and my painting, Maxine is always in my mind. What would she say about my arguments for the virtue of copying as one way to paint and think about the world? I intend to discuss this with her one of these days, but I am still trying to understand why this kind of painting is so compelling to me at this stage of my life. I think age has gotten me to think more about preservation, about what I've learned, what my life and writing have achieved, and more broadly, what has happened historically in education and society during my time. In education, I've participated in at least three cycles of reform and have seen shifts from open, student-oriented, and experiential learning to more closed, product-oriented schooling. Throughout these cycles, the persistence of failure in poor communities and the questioning of the viability of public education systems have been persistent. In our society, as in the world, the growth of fear, cultural anxiety, and suspicion is endemic. Growing older at a time when there seems to be no large vision of healing or sense of hope and at a time when it is hard to see much progress in democratic education or society is troubling. I fear that the world I will leave behind will be the graveyard of the hope for decency and justice that has driven my life. The idea that the world is locked in a condition of endless warfare is demoralizing. At this time, I find myself working for the cycle to swing back toward decency. I long for what in *Journey to the West* was the renewed ascendancy of the Positive side. I also worry about how to age in hard and sad times; how to bend under stormy conditions and still show strength and refuse to be uprooted.

These thoughts have become symbolized for me by bamboo and have led to another flight of imagination based in my painting Chinese and my essentially silent companionship with the children I paint with.

ENJOYING PINE AND BAMBOO
I treasure what front eaves face
and all that north windows frame.

Bamboo winds lavish out windows,
pine colors exquisite beyond eaves.

I gather it all in to isolate mystery,
thoughts fading to their source.

Others may feel nothing in all this,
but it's perfectly open to me now:

such kindred natures need share
neither root nor form nor gesture.

I enrolled at the Joseph Fine Arts School for a third semester and returned to my place at the table, only this time I knew all the pre-painting rituals and was ready when Joseph came over with a painting of bamboo for me to copy. As usual, he told me to plunge in and continue painting bamboo. I wasn't as hesitant as I'd been before, and it looked simple to me then. Only I soon discovered that it was very difficult to breathe life into a bamboo, to have it move with wind, to have it serene on a quiet day, to have it bursting with leaves or barren or budding. Painting bamboo was considered a separate branch of painting as difficult as calligraphy and very close in style and technique to the art of writing.

My fellow students came in, and all but Pearl and Lynn sat at their places. Pearl did not show, and Joseph told me she chose to come at another time. Joseph taught two one-hour classes a day five days a week and six classes on Saturday. Lynn was moved to a table in the next room where the more advanced students were painting. There were two new students who sat across the table, and their faces were hidden by the easels.

Fen and Hui Ying had also moved to bamboo painting, while Chen remained with monkeys and pandas a bit longer. The two new students were started on monkeys.

Fen was her usual exuberant, confident self and jumped right into painting bamboo. While she was hard at work, one of her strokes bled, since she had a bit too much water on her brush. This

misstep surprisingly shook her confidence. It seemed to me that she was on the verge of tears. Joseph naturally came to her rescue and with a few deft strokes turned one stalk of bamboo into two, letting the gray ink that bled from her brush shade the second stalk.

Hui Ying seemed much more relaxed and in control of things this semester. She still tried to get her painting exactly right and came pretty close—close enough to please her and elicit praise from Joseph.

Chen pouted. Despite his age, he wanted to be up with the rest. Joseph gently pushed him into painting panda bears with the concession of giving him a painting of a panda eating a bamboo stalk. Chen was quite content with that, since he too was painting bamboo in a way.

Painting bamboo provided me with a greater challenge than the other work I was doing, and I found myself working very hard to develop a minimal level of mastery. Joseph kept providing me with more and more complex paintings of clusters of bamboo in different weather conditions and with different shadings, which meant mixing ink and water in many differing proportions. It seemed that Joseph was presenting me with more difficult challenges than he was the children, though I may be flattering myself.

However, we all began with the same simple lessons. Painting a bamboo stalk with leaves requires deeper knowledge of brush-work than does monkeys or pandas. There are two challenges that require new strokes: painting the stems and then the leaves. Joseph demonstrated these strokes to each of us separately, inking the brush first for the stem. The bamboo stem has many sections, starting from short at one end and then getting longer and longer in the middle and then getting shorter again at the other, root end. Each section is made with a single brushstroke. First the brush has to be prepared with a little bit of water and ink. Too much ink produces large black spots; too little ink creates too bare an effect. Too much water bleeds into the paper, creating a halo effect around your work. This mostly dry brush is then held perpendicular to the paper and pressed down. The brush is then dragged down the length of the section by moving your arm, not your wrist. At the end of the section, the brush is pressed again and then removed from the paper. The pressing produces the slight broadening of the stem at its joint area. After one section is completed, another one is done, moving all the way down the stalk.

Joseph's stroke was graceful, but before he was done with one section I started worrying about how to load the brush. I tried hard to remember exactly what he did in both inking and painting and felt quite nervous about my performance. I pretended to just jump in but took a moment to watch Fen and Hui Ying. Fen took to painting the stalk without any problem. She got the mixture right, or I imagined she did, since her result was a clear, convincing, graceful bamboo stalk. Hui Ying also got the ink right, but she had a harder time with the stroke. She didn't move the brush with the same ease as Fen. It was as if she were fighting it, trying to hold it back from making a mess. I thoroughly identified with her. Neither of them had any trouble using her arm to move the brush along the paper.

Joseph glanced at me, and I knew it was time to get to work. I still had not given up the ingrained habit of worrying about making mistakes or creating an ugly painting. Not surprisingly, I put too much ink on the brush, and my bamboo looked dark and lumpy.

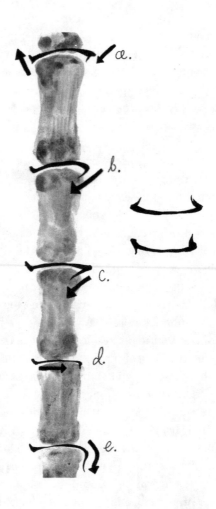

I pressed down too hard on the brush, so my first effort led to a stumpy bamboo stalk with knobby lumps at the end of each section. Joseph came over, smiled, and said it was a good effort. He then slowly showed me how to move the brush one more time and remarked that bamboo came in all sizes and shapes. My second effort was better, but there was too little water and too little ink on the brush. However, the effect was great: The bamboo looked as though it had some dimensionality, since the stroke left white space in the center of each section. I tried a third time, almost getting it. This time, there was just a little too much water and a blot on one of the sections. The children and I were painting away. I saw them smiling at their own work and caught myself smiling and relaxing. It was like gliding through water—I was totally immersed in the act of painting for several minutes. It was in me and all around me, and I felt childlike for a moment. Or at least I felt what adults like to call childlike. It felt closely akin to meditation. The lesson ended with me feeling refreshed and giddy. Judy noticed it when she picked me up and joked that I had better be careful lest I forget about the troubles in my university program and walk away from everything whistling. Of course, she wouldn't have minded if I did. Things had been getting very intense at the university, and it took me several hours to unwind at home on nonpainting days.

After the stems came the leaves—another brushstroke altogether. The leaf is also made with a single stroke, which is described in *Chinese Painting Techniques* by Alison Stilwell Cameron:

> *Mix some . . . ink and water, making a darker shade [than used for the stem] this time. . . . With the underside of your arm and wrist*

resting on the table, hold the brush so the handle is slanted and the tip is pointed towards the top of the paper. Lay the entire length of the brush hairs down on the paper. Twist the handle slightly to the left and right to give a blunt end. Now pull straight toward you, lifting the brush gradually until only the tip is still touching the paper. Pause and then flick the tip of the brush up off the paper to end with a point. The arm and wrist must rest on the table with the hand and fingers manipulating the brush; do not use your whole arm. Slant the brush far enough out from your hand so that there will be room to bring it back to the vertical position at the end of the stroke.

As usual, Joseph demonstrated and we followed in our own ways. I found myself an irregular painter of leaves. Sometimes they turned out well; other times they were lumpy and blunt at both ends or blotted or shaky. As the lessons on painting bamboo continued, leaves and stems came together, along with branches, to make bamboo groves, and bamboo moving in the wind, and I became free of constant anxiety and the pressure and complications of my work life.

For me, there was more to painting bamboos than just taking another step toward working on a full landscape. Bamboo represents peace, health, and long life, and that soothed and nurtured me.

Every Chinese market or flower store on Clement Street sold live bamboo, either in lengths up to seven or eight feet or in short bundles of "lucky" stalks wrapped in red ribbons. There was also potted bamboo, some stalks twisting around one another like strands of double and triple helixes.

As my lessons continued, I took to spending time at the Asian Art Museum of San Francisco and was profoundly moved by paintings of bamboo or that contained bamboo. They moved with the wind or sat calmly on a sunny day. Wherever they were, they were a presence. There was one particular bamboo painting that was about four feet by six feet. The bamboo was absolutely alive, graceful and strained by some storm, yet holding tenaciously to the earth. There were no depictions of either the earth or the storm in the painting, just the bamboo that told the whole story by itself. I understood what Joseph meant when he remarked one day that painting bamboo can be a life's work.

Consequently, I set out on another lateral journey provoked by my painting Chinese. I decided to study the meaning of bamboo in Chinese painting and culture and began to read whatever I could find that mentioned painting bamboo. In the seventeenth-century classic of traditional Chinese painting, *The Mustard Seed Garden Manual of Painting*, I discovered that bamboo painting was a special branch of painting, somewhere on the boundary of calligraphy. It was considered a form that required special skill and delicacy and a deep understanding of the nature of the human heart. According to Chieh Tzu Yuan Hua Chuan, author of the book:

> *Where bamboos are painted in the wind, their stems are stretched out and taut and the leaves give the impression of disorder, their joints bend, and startled rooks fly out from the foliage. Bamboos in rain bend. How could it be otherwise? In fair weather, bamboo leaves compose themselves in pairs. . . . A cluster of young bamboos should be composed on a foundation of strong forked*

branches with small leaves at the tips of the branches, joined by groups of larger leaves in the body of the plant. Bamboos laden with dew resemble those in the rain. In fair weather they do not bend; in rain they do not stand erect; heavy with dew, their tops bend and almost touch the lower branches. . . . There are certain general faults in the painting of bamboo that one should remember to avoid. First of all and basically, shih *(structural integrity) should always be the main concern, but unless heart (Hsin— heart mind) and idea (i) are attuned, there can be no good results. It is essential to have serenity, something that can only arise from a tranquil soul. Avoid making stems like drum-sticks. Avoid making joints of equal length. Avoid lining up the bamboos like a fence. Avoid placing the leaves all to one side. Avoid making them . . . dragonfly wings, or like the fingers of an outstretched hand, or like the crisscrossing of a net, or like the leaves of the peach or willow. At the moment of putting brush to paper, do not hesitate. From the deepest recesses of the heart should come the power that propels the brush to action.*

Learning about bamboo introduced me to the complex spiritual component at the center of Chinese landscape painting. Most of the early manuals on Chinese painting are grounded in Taoism, and most of the Chinese painters I have studied are influenced by the Tao. In Taoism, people are admonished to respect and honor nature and understand its contradictions. Nature is a force to be witnessed and entered into with reverence, not something to be modified and controlled for human use. These tensions within the natural world, which are also metaphors for the tensions in human life, have been issues in Chinese thinking since the seventh century BC, when Lao Tzu is said to have written the *Tao Te Ching*. According to Taoism, people should strive toward effortless action and an acceptance of contradictions. A classic example of this, drawn from verse 78 of the *Tao Te Ching,* is the action of water that flows effortlessly down to the lowest level and yet wears down the hardest rock:

> *Nothing in the world is softer and weaker than water;*
> *But, for attacking the hard and strong, there is nothing*
>   *Like it!*
> *For nothing can take its place.*
> *That the weak overcomes the strong, and the soft*
>   *Overcomes the hard,*
> *This is something known by all, and practiced*
>   *By none.*

One goal of the Chinese painter's brushwork is to be effortless, uniting hand, heart, mind, and nature. Joseph's avoidance of pressure, his soft voice, gentle guiding of one's work, and subtle support, which does not involve explicit praise so much as examination of the virtues of one's work, all aim toward helping his students move toward painting effortlessly. I find the children take to such effortless work without having to be tutored, especially when they are not criticized by adults or other children. One major reason for this is that they are free to explore the world through their art and simply have fun doing it. It is a form of youthful innocence that allows children to ask the most unlikely questions and try the most difficult work without being self-conscious. Even Hui Ying has developed an effortless way of working and accepting instruction from Joseph. It is a gift the children need in the competitive school environments they have to navigate.

Except for a few unpredictable moments of effortless work, I was the only one in the class who was still self-conscious, overly analytical, and nervous about getting things right. Yet when I went home to Point Arena and painted by myself, I found it easier to accept this new, somewhat Taoist way and painted effortlessly. Still, I was uncertain about the whole enterprise and knew that I was still under pressure in my work and couldn't make the bridge between painting and work effectively. I hoped that would come when I left the university.

Reading the *Tao Te Ching* inspired me to learn more about the meaning of Taoist symbols and in particular bamboo, which I was still painting. Bamboo grows easily and does not need much care. It grows quickly and energetically and remains fresh and green even during the cold season. It is hollow inside, which in Taoist-Buddhist thinking connotes the value of being void, of the "Positive emptiness" that Sun Wukong was awakened to. That void is symbolic of freedom from worldly contamination, of purity. Bamboo is on the Positive side.

Bamboo's hollow core enables it to sway and bend in even the most severe storms, and it never becomes uprooted. Its ability to survive under extreme difficulty has endeared it to poets and painters, and it often is used as a metaphor for human survival. Learning to bend, sway, and yield without breaking or losing your roots or having your substance destroyed during troubled times is a major human challenge, one that I have faced a number of times. For me, painting bamboo has become a way of reflecting on staying rooted during hard times. As I continued my lessons with Joseph, I began to develop metaphors drawn from my painting experiences that continue to help me think and feel my way through facing the consequences of aging. It supports my need for a secular spiritualism, one that faces death as an absolute ending of life, a frightening prospect, yet dignifies aging and living knowing that it will end incomplete, as will many other things I do. After all, life ends with the incompleteness of death. This scares me, yet I have no choice but to accept it as inevitable.

There is no limit to the range and variety of bamboo that one can paint. However, getting the bamboo right, making it come alive and seem active, is a complex, difficult challenge. I don't have any illusions about ever mastering bamboo painting, but the act of painting it has become a form of liberation. It is a challenge that can continue until the end of my life, never completed, always nurturing.

I am certainly neither unique nor special in finding the symbolic, poetic, and spiritual value of nature personally transforming, but it is definitely an awakening that has deepened my life.

I questioned a boy under the pine trees.
"My master went herb gathering,"
   he says
He is somewhere on the mountain-side,
So deep in the clouds I can't tell where.

—JIA DAO

Joseph has been as important to me as the children have been. He has become a mentor, a master teacher in a way, perhaps Buddhist, I have not encountered before. After learning from him for several years, I asked if he would be willing to tell me something of his story, how he learned to paint and how he learned to teach. To my surprise, he said yes.

Joseph began his story when he was living in China during the Cultural Revolution, which started when he was ten years old in 1966. During middle school, he carried Mao's "Little Red Book" and had to learn Mao's political ideas. After this formal schooling ended, he was required to work in a factory. All of the colleges in China were closed, and there was a massive attempt to "reeducate the intellectuals" and send all of the potential young college students to the fields or factories to work with "the people."

Joseph was assigned to learn jade carving in an art factory. I asked him what an art factory was, and he explained that it was a place where everything from dishes, cups, vases, screens, silk hangings, ink paintings, and rice bowls were created and hand-painted on a massive scale. He spent six years there.

He said that at that time, young people had a great deal of energy. The day began with group exercise and martial arts. Then there was work at the factory, and in the evening there were sketching and art classes. That's where he was initially trained.

After the Cultural Revolution ended and colleges reopened, he attended the Nanjing Art Institute for four years, learning painting, sculpture, and calligraphy. In 1982, Joseph and about twenty-five other students were kept on to teach. He taught at the college for five years. There was also an opening to Western art, and Joseph took advantage of that opportunity by traveling to the United States to study at the Academy of Art College in San Francisco.

A few things Joseph told me provided insight into the way he went about teaching at the school and helped me understand what it meant to be a student in a traditional Chinese art school. He said that in China he spent four hours in the morning learning art, and then in the afternoon he spent two or three hours learning poetry, culture, and philosophy. At night, he did homework. According to Joseph, "College was very fun, you work hard, you feel, every day you achieve more knowledge."

He emphasized that he had very good teachers. He said, "Teachers in China take a very great responsibility in the latter generation. They teach very seriously. They don't let you do whatever you want. They say, Let's carve, you learn from me, okay? You do what we ask you to do, and after school, you can do whatever you want. We had very serious training. We did sketch, sculpture, still life, gouache, acrylic, landscape, jade carving, clay, and woodcutting." These are all aspects of the visual arts that Joseph is willing to teach at the fine arts school. He concluded by saying, "School always opened my mind."

Joseph has studied three different ways to paint: traditional Chinese in many of its modes, social realism, and contemporary Western. In his own work, he moves from one style to another and mixes and matches them. In his school, he has chosen to concentrate solely on traditional Chinese painting. The mission of the school goes beyond painting to passing on aspects of traditional Chinese culture to Chinese and Chinese American children growing up in the United States. In this he has the support of many parents and many people in the community. One day he shared a scrapbook with me. It showed the work of many of his students who began, as did Fen, Hui Ying, Chen, Lynn, and Pearl, at a very young age and stayed with him throughout their high school careers. Many, if not most, of these older students are in college, at Stanford, the University of California at Berkeley, Pomona, and other first-class institutions. During one summer session, I met a number of them who had come back to take additional lessons during their vacations. They understand, as does Joseph, that learning to paint Chinese is a lifelong journey that affects their ways of seeing and being in the world. And I have come to see and feel it the same way.

THE CATARACT OF LUH SHAN
Westward I ascend the Peak of Incense Burner;
Southward I see the mighty waterfall.
It plunges three hundred chang *down the mountain,*

And froths for miles in the rapids below.
As wind-driven snow speed the waters,
Like a white rainbow spanning the dark,
I wonder if Heaven's River had fallen from above
To course through the mid-sky of clouds.

Long I lift my gaze—Oh, prodigious force!
How majestic the creation of gods!
Unwavering before the ocean winds that blow,
Glaring at the faint moon over the river,
Profusely it sprays the sky
And drenches the green mountain walls.
The swift torrents boil over giant rocks;
The flying water scatters a mist of ethereal gems.

O mountains of renown that I adore,
You fill my heart with deep repose.
No longer need I take the portion of precious stones,
You can wash away the earth stains from my face.
Let me be with the things I love,
And leave the world of man forever.

—LI PO

For the rest of my third semester, the children and I painted fish
and birds as well as bamboo. Learning to paint fish and birds was a
way of introducing me to using Chinese watercolors and learning
to mix paints in a traditional way. Green is a common color, and
Joseph showed us how to mix it from blue and yellow, how to cre-

ate shades of green by using more or less water, and how to mix in a bit of red or brown to get a particular tint. There are some paintings where at least half a dozen shades and tints of green are used.

I liked the fish painting, which tested my capacity to paint in yellow, shades of green, and plain black ink. To supplement my knowledge of fish movement and color, each Wednesday before the lesson I went to a fish store that was down the block next to the Taiwan Restaurant. At first, I wasn't aware of it. The signs were in Chinese, and at the entrance is a little shop that sells bamboo, orchids, and other flowers. I loved to study the range and variety of the bamboo and take in the colors of the orchids. However, I noticed a funny fishy smell coming from what I thought was the back room of the flower shop. One day, when I had time to kill (Joseph did not like people to come too early), I decided to go into that back room and found myself surrounded by tanks and tanks of fish. The store was larger than Joseph's whole school and sold scores of varieties of fresh- and salt-water fish, anemones, underwater plants, turtles, and crustaceans. On the second floor, they also sold a variety of aquariums, fish food, pumps, water filters, heaters, and other accessories.

My visits to the store enhanced my renderings of the fish paintings Joseph presented to us. However, no matter how much I tried, my fish just didn't have the life of Fen's fish or the perfect and steady line of Hui Ying's. And they took to color boldly, playfully experimenting with yellows, golds, reds, and oranges. I labored at my fish, knowing what I wanted to achieve but hardly ever getting there. Fen took to saying quietly that my work was nice. She may have sensed my insecurity and was trying to encourage me. She was acting like Joseph, and I was the struggling child. My wife, Judy, and some of my students also supported me and gave what I often took as kind but insincere praise of my work. Yet on reflection, my paintings weren't that bad. It's just that I wanted to become a master overnight when it really would take a lifetime of effort to achieve work even approximating that of the masters.

Looking to the masters might have been part of my problem. I bought books of paintings by the greatest Chinese masters during the time of fish painting and started copying some master paintings of fish at home. Some of them seemed so simple and elegant, and initially I felt they would be easy to reproduce and embellish. But as I painted them, the sophistication of line, the slight twisting of the body, the positioning of the fins and tails so that you could feel the water they were gliding through, were beyond my skill. Trying to paint the masters gave me insight into what Joseph meant by painting with your heart. I was not yet secure enough to let my heart flow into my work.

The children had an easier time putting their hearts to work. Joseph gently encouraged them to paint from a model but to make it their own. As the third semester went on, their work became more lively and skillful. It was wonderful to see Fen, Hui Ying, and Chen buried in their work. I got the feeling that they were even tempted to taste the colors and paint their own hands and faces. It was the unity of child and work that I'd seen when I was teaching kindergarten. At moments, the children were totally absorbed and at the same time totally free.

After fish, we spent time painting birds. I had some trouble painting birds. You had to catch them in flight or sitting on a

branch or running across a field. They had to have weight and movement. It was not easy, yet it was fun.

I did my best with birds, but my heart wasn't in it, and Joseph sensed it. I wanted to move on to landscape and skip the birds but went with the school's program for the rest of my third semester and signed up for another. Joseph told me I was ready to start on landscape next semester.

∘ ∘ ∘

There are basically two traditional styles of Chinese landscape painting: the freehand impression style (*xieyi*) and the detailed, elaborate brushwork style (*gongbi*). The distinction between these styles was articulated by the art critic Dong Qichang during the Ming dynasty (AD 1368–1644), though they had been practiced as early as the Tang dynasty (AD 618–907). The freehand style is also called the Southern or Literary style, and the detailed is the Northern or Academic style. *Xieyi* means "write ideas," and the brushstrokes are closer to the strokes in calligraphy. They tend to be simple, bold, and flowing: somewhat impressionistic, paying little attention to detail. This style was created by "literati," who were also poets and developed the tradition of calligraphing poems directly on their paintings. The poems and the paintings work together to create a whole, which is foreign to Western classical painting. *Gonbi* is a more formal style, with fine, carefully controlled brushwork that pays attention to details. *Xieyi* artists normally signed their paintings "Written by," while *gonbi* painters signed them "Made by."

In the early twentieth century, with the establishment of the Republic of China, many of the techniques and ideas of Western painting were integrated into Chinese painting. This fusion movement, initiated mostly by *xieyi* painters based in traditional painting, was centered in the Shanghai area. Joseph comes from Jiang Su, and some of his and Janny's teachers were from that school. When introducing beginning students to landscape painting, he uses what he calls impression style, which seems to me to be a simplified version of *xieyi* style that uses outlining.

At the beginning of the new semester, I was the only student in the beginners' class painting landscape. Fen worked on flowers and insects; Hui Ying moved on to birds and bamboo-bird compositions. Chen was painting bamboo and fish. An interesting incident happened with Chen the first day of class. Before Joseph had a chance to give him a painting, he came over and looked at the landscape on my easel. He went to Joseph and demanded once more that he paint what I was painting. If I could do landscape, he could do landscape. Joseph smiled and said he certainly would be able to do landscape, but not yet. He then gave Chen a painting of a menacing-looking fish, and that seemed to content him, as the issue dissipated quickly.

I thought that if this had happened in my kindergarten, I would have let Chen try the landscape and praised whatever he came up with. The desire to reach out and try something an adult was doing, to tackle a difficult task and be able to accomplish something with it, would in my view be a valuable learning experience. It would encourage boldness and experimentation and could result in a very interesting, if somewhat impressionist, painting.

I shared my thoughts with Joseph, and he commented that it was an interesting idea, but it was not right for him to teach as

I would, as he had a different program. He was worried that Chen would develop bad brush habits and an exalted sense of his painting abilities if he tried to paint a complex landscape. It was better to distract him and let him develop in a way that was consistent with his current state of development. He then explained to me that though I was painting with the children and doing the same work they were, he felt I was ready to do more complex things. I protested and explained that the children's skill level was much greater than mine. He brushed that off. Skill in a specific sense did not interest him. It was thought, heart, and understanding. Once the handling of the brush became relatively comfortable, the skills could develop in many different ways. He felt that the complex task of composing a landscape was suitable for me at this stage and not for this five-year-old.

I don't remember the first landscape Joseph put on my easel, but it excited me. It's hard to understand my obsession with landscape, but I'm sure it has to do with my love of the landscape around my home in Point Arena and the joy I feel walking through the woods or spending time at the ocean or along one of the rivers that make up our watershed. It purifies me and calms me down after working in the city. It is the sounds as well that feel so nurturing—the birds, the waves, the fog, and the rain. Even the storms are wonderful. Landscapes speak to me, and painting them provides me with an intimacy with nature that equals the actual experience and allows me to add the element of imagination so I can people the landscape in any way I want.

All of the early landscapes I painted had certain characteristics in common. There were rocks and trees in the foreground and mountains of just about every shape and form in the mid- and background. At first, Joseph suggested I just paint what I saw and went on to work with the other students. I looked at the painting and then at my paper. Where to begin? Should I start with the rocks or the trees? Should I sketch in the mountains in the background and leave space for the boulders and trees in the foreground? If I worked on the foreground, should I begin with trees or rocks and bushes?

I had faced this problem before when I tried to sketch Western master paintings and ended up with a mess. I had no overall sense of how to organize my work and frequently found it necessary to squeeze in buildings or hills or trees because I had filled up my paper with oversize, out-of-proportion parts of the original. Before I began studying with Joseph, I painted with abandon, disregarding composition and any semblance of reality. It was a bit like finger painting. Often I would throw some paint on a canvas and watch it drip down the surface using a Western-style easel. Then I followed the forms that emerged and made houses, animals, people, and monsters, shaping them according to themes that were on my mind. They were neither impressionist nor expressionist. They were intuitive, untutored statements that pleased me in the doing and were, more often than not, disappointments in the execution. It was at that time, almost twenty years before I stumbled into the Joseph Fine Arts School, that I determined to take painting lessons someday.

My first efforts at landscape were intriguing. Joseph suggested I outline everything beforehand and not use any colors until all the ink was done and dry. First I began painting the rocks,

then I tried to begin with a tree, then a mountain. Joseph observed my effort and always commented, praising one or two details of a work, never judging the whole, but making specific suggestions. His praise was very specific—"These rocks are well grained but could have more cracks," "That tree trunk bends well, but try to make the bottom feel like it is rooted in the ground," "This mountain fits in well, but next time make it a bit more gray like it is far away," "The leaves here need to be filled in more."

The children always listened carefully to what Joseph was telling me and perhaps learned more from his suggestions than I did. I noticed how passionately the young ones wanted to learn, to absorb as much as they could and then practice it. It reminded me of what a Navajo educator once told me about how children learned to weave the extraordinary rugs that their culture has produced. Children are given small looms and are encouraged to sit next to adult weavers and watch them at work. Children, when unencumbered by adult demands and channeling educational structures, are extraordinary watchers and learn through what they see and experience. It seemed clear to me that the children were learning about landscape through what Joseph was teaching me.

As I began to feel part of the landscapes I was copying, I began to pay attention to details before paying attention to the whole composition. What this did was get me to look more carefully at the originals. How was that rock rendered? What shade of black or gray was used? How did the graining develop? Were all of the rocks rendered in the same way? How did the rocks relate to one another? I also began to comprehend the structure of the landscapes, how the masters put them together to become slightly discordant but harmonious wholes, and Joseph encouraged me to feel them as I observed and painted. He was gently pushing me into the spirit of Chinese painting and repeated several times that the feeling and spirit with which I painted was more important than the technique, while insisting I still pay attention to the technique.

Once, while I was clumsily attempting a mountain, my brush sprayed a few blots next to the mountain in a blank space. When Joseph came over, I told him about the mess and he just smiled and said the blots were not a mess, they were birds. He then took the brush gently out of my hand and painted delicate lines emerging from the dots—wings. Indeed, they were birds flying somewhere in the space between the foreground rocks and trees and the distant mountains. It reminded me of the way I used to paint, following the flow of the paint.

This playful aspect of painting gave me a glimpse of what Joseph meant by the spirit of painting. It was not a matter of making an exact copy, it was getting the flow of the painting right with the assistance of a traditional work and a mentor. It was a manifestation of what Taoists called *tzu-jan,* naturalness or harmony in one's actions, and was somewhat akin to what Mihalya Csikszentmihalyi called "flow." Flow exists at a time of optimal performance when idea, effort, goal, body, and mind are all effortlessly united in performance. These days, painting Chinese, I feel that one goal is to get to that moment of wholeness and joy. I knew it would be a long struggle to acquire the skills and understanding necessary to develop the sustained grace and effortlessness that can be described as participating in the Tao.

The more I read about Chinese landscape painting, the clearer its intimate connection with Taoism became. In *The Way of the Brush,* Fritz van Briessen cites this parable from Zhuangzi as a way of introducing the relationship between landscape painting and Taoism. Evidently, there was "a certain 'man from Ying' who had a scab on his nose no thicker than the wing of a housefly. He sent for a stonemason to have it cut away. The stonemason wielded his adze with such skill that afterward the man's nose was quite unharmed, and he had not even changed color."

Van Briessen continues: "These and other passages . . . suggest that, although technical skill alone is not enough, a mastery of technique leads the artist beyond the material limitations of this world to a higher knowledge, a perception of Tao. So skill is not simply a necessary step toward Tao but part of it. The command of technique leads, through assiduous practice, through the reconciling of the inward and the outward, through the conquest of material difficulties, toward a final liberation."

Finally, van Briessen turns to *shan-shui,* landscape painting: "Translated literally the two syllables mean 'mountain and water,' opposing what is hard, solid, and resistant in mountain and rock to the feminine element of water, which is yielding, pliant, and changing. Water obeys the laws of gravity, and yet . . . its ceaseless flux forms mountains and rocks and occasionally conquers them. Out of these fundamental opposites, Chinese landscape painting was born. It is an attempt to show in visual terms the identity of Yin and Yang, their interplay and their unity at a higher level. . . . This idea pervades the whole of Chinese landscape painting at all stages."

The lofty, perhaps unachievable goal of painting effortlessly has not yet come to me, and throughout the early stages of my lessons, the idea of the unity of opposites was not much on my mind. I still struggled with the simplest lines and the most basic landscapes. I tried to make sense out of the whole and figure out how to piece it together. I was copying mechanically more than painting effortlessly, though there were moments when it all came together in a rock or the peak of a mountain or the leaves of a small tree in the corner of what to me was a crude attempt at a landscape. The children were closer to obtaining the flow I thought and read about without being inhibited by my self-conscious inquiries into the history and meaning of what I was doing. By the end of the semester, Fen had moved on to lovely flower compositions. Chen was forging ahead with determination, seemingly unconcerned about lines that were too broad and colors that bled. His work was compelling, full of energy and life. However, Hui Ying's commitment to painting seemed to be waning, and she worked listlessly. Joseph spent time encouraging her, but her heart wasn't in it. Perhaps she needed to be pushed or thrown into a competitive situation in order to motivate herself to perform. It was certainly possible that the high-stakes testing and pressured schooling she was undergoing made her too tired and fearful of learning without being judged. I don't know any of this for sure and of course couldn't ask, even indirectly, without violating my position as just another student. It was not my business in this context to query other students about their motives and lives. Our relationship was casual, and our painting was individualized, a matter between each of us individually and Joseph in conversation with the masters.

You came, Sir,
  from my old village—
You must know
  all the village affairs;
Tell me,
  was the winter-plum in
  flower
Before my gauze window
  On the day you left?

—WANG WEI

By my fourth semester, I had become part of the landscape of the school. Parents nodded at me. Joseph had told a few of the older students that I was a professor and a writer, and every once in a while they asked me a question about getting into college or about my work. One Wednesday, Grace, a sixth-grade student who was in a more advanced painting class, was doing her homework in the outer room while waiting to be picked up by her mother. I had never said a word to her before, but she called me over as I was about to leave and asked me to help her with her math homework. Of course I agreed, thoroughly confident I could still do sixth-grade work. After all, I had minored in math at Harvard in the 1950s.

As best as I can reconstruct it, the problem, which was in the advanced challenges section of Grace's algebra book, was:

Given a *and* b *as labeled on the diagram, find the length* x.

I sat down and started to work on the problem. Clearly, the characteristics of right triangles had to be involved in the solution. I began to fiddle around with the Pythagorean theorem and with labeling all of the other sides of the diagram. And then I panicked. Grace was watching me, and waiting parents were watching me. I felt sure that Joseph was watching me, too, but the next week he reassured me that he wasn't paying attention and that the event wasn't important. But it was important to me.

I could not develop a solution to the problem and gave up. I apologized to Grace for my ineptness and muttered something about old age and forgetfulness as I left the storefront with my head down. I had failed miserably in their presence, and it humiliated me. My calm cover had been blown; I had slipped back into that tense, insecure, competitive mode that Joseph's teaching and my painting had begun to liberate me from.

During the next week, I carried a copy of the problem in my pocket, and the more I tried to solve it, the harder it seemed. I even entertained the idea that the textbook had an error or that I had copied it down incorrectly. Most of geometry had slipped out of my mind, as I never had occasion to use it. I behaved the way many of my students do when they experience initial failure. Failure provides frustration, which leads to additional panic and reinforcement of the feeling of failure. Finally, I asked some friends to help me with the problem, but geometry had slipped away from them, too. It would have been wiser for me to ask some sixth graders for help. In fact, I asked Grace about the problem a few weeks later, and she told me that one of her classmates had helped her solve the problem the evening she had asked me.

This was not the first time I had forgotten something I had once known. Judy and I had noticed that for the past several years, names, dates, and places were harder for us to remember. When we shared memories and reminisced, there were gaps in our stories. Sequences of events were forgotten; it was hard to remember who was present during demonstrations or dinners or at conferences and meetings. In one of my books, which I wrote in the late 1990s, I told a story about how I met a particular important educator during a community struggle in Harlem in the 1960s. I asked that person to check my writing, and she said the account was completely inaccurate. She had a different, equally plausible memory. Neither of us had a way to verify the truth, and since I was the older, I deferred to her younger and fresher memory, though it still doesn't seem right to me. None of this struggle with increasingly impressionistic memories of the past was crippling, but it was noticeable, and I began to think more about memory and aging.

Being among the children, I also wondered about the memories of five-, six-, and seven-year-olds. They had personal histories just as I had and most likely constructed stories and myths out of their experiences. I wondered what Fen or Chen or the other children would remember about their experience at Joseph's when they were eight or nine. I felt confident that whatever they remembered and however they reconstructed their experiences at the school, they would take away skills that would reside in their muscles and images that would reside in their memories. Still, the internal lives of children are a mystery to me, even after teaching for about fifty years. I've never been among children who did not surprise me with what they remembered and with how they interpreted their past. It seems as if looking back comes with being conscious.

However, the distance from past experiences that comes from being older has a way of eroding and shaping memory that is perhaps quite different from a child's memory. It is intriguing what memory loses, preserves, or distorts throughout life but perhaps more dramatically in old age. Wang Wei's poem at the head of this section reminded me of the memories I have of my childhood home and how, every once in a while, I wonder about what is happening there now. The neighborhood is different, the people who live there are strangers, but the building stands and the spirit of our family life in that home is still alive in my memory. I struggle to remember the details of the apartment I spent seventeen years living in and sometimes wonder if the sparrows are still coming to nest in the lone tree in front of the house. And if the seedpods we used to open up and put on our noses to make us look like Pinocchio still fall from the tree every September.

A few years ago, I visited the house, and the numbers my grandfather nailed up over the front door the day we moved in sometime in 1940 were still there. However, my little science lab and writing space in the basement had become the assembly room of a West Indian Pentecostal church. The current occupants of the house graciously let me come in and look around. The first thing I looked for was the mezuzah that my father had put on the lintel of the door to our downstairs apartment. It was still there, painted over maybe a dozen times. I pointed it out to the minister who lived in what used to be our apartment, and he told me he would take it off and give it to me. I surprised myself by refusing, wanting only to take away the memories of having lived there. Besides, it was there to bless the house, and I couldn't imagine any reason to take away that blessing.

These days, I find my memory tested constantly by painting Chinese. I have to depend upon memory to understand and practice what Joseph teaches. The dilemma is that Joseph does not have a linear curriculum, there is no textbook, it's impossible to take notes, and when he comes by to offer help or demonstrate something, it happens so quickly and casually that it's hard to remember when I get home and work on my own. This seems to be less of a problem for the children. They get the gestalt, go right to work, and seem to have an immediate and fluid relationship to their work that eludes me. And, as I've noticed in many young children I've taught, when left alone to integrate what they've learned without being pushed or prodded by adults, they take in what is demonstrated and apply it without pain or reflection. It was a delight to see my painting partners learn from Joseph. They let him take their brushes and demonstrate a stroke or add a detail to their work. They listened when he pointed out something they could work on. Then, with the same smile indicating "I got it" that I have observed on the faces of young children who all of a sudden "get it," they charge right in and apply and practice what they have learned. Fen adds a touch here, a touch there, always with a smile. And Chen, with the wicked smile I imagine Monkey King has, gets right to the painting, humming to himself.

Then there is clumsy, hesitant, analytic me. I analyze Joseph's indirect lessons and try to remember what he did, or at least try to reconstruct them mentally, before returning to my painting. During those early days of my lessons, I felt insecure and vulnerable facing Joseph and the children, yet they did nothing to intimidate me and were all kind, generous, and friendly. No challenge, no criticism, no threat. The problems I faced learning, relaxing, and painting came with me. They reminded me of a copy of a Goya print I bought in Paris in 1958 and have had hanging on the wall wherever I've worked for the past forty-seven years. Its title is *Buen Viage,* and it shows a winged monster flying off on a voyage with all of his old demons playing and carousing on his back. I simply cannot run away from myself and still carry all of the baggage of my personal history and habits with me as I set out on this new adventure. I am still the same militant, imperfect, joyful and melancholy, confused, knowledgeable, sometimes determined and sometimes hesitant person keenly aware of living in an uncertain and often unjust world that I want to change. *Buen viage* indeed. I had a lot of unlearning to do before painting Chinese with ease and unmitigated joy.

Since Joseph teaches based on needs that arise organically while we paint, there is no telling what one might learn any particular day. If painting is flowing, he stays out of the way, though sometimes he goes out of his way to point out an aspect of the work he likes. What's even more useful is that he describes precisely what is good about it. A lot of his teaching is in the details of students' work. His praise helps me reflect on my own work. I knew that I couldn't yet make the whole landscape cohere, but those details he pointed out were models, examples of brief moments of connection. For example, once I was working on a mountain scene with tall, craggy peaks in the background and boulders and trees in the foreground. Joseph never said anything until I finished the landscape. He then looked at the whole and pointed out a cluster of large rocks in the lower right foreground of the work and said they were particularly effective. He pointed to one large rock and said that it really looked as though it were rooted in the earth and that the reason was that I made the grass and bushes around it look as if they were being pushed back by its presence. He made no comment on the painting as a whole but gave me a model, in my own work, of decent painting. I had to agree and remember how much I had liked those rocks when they were finished. However, the challenge was to remember how I did them and to be able to incorporate that ease and grace into future work. I had to reconstruct the combination of ink and water used, the way the brushstrokes were made, the feelings I had when painting the rocks, and the model rocks I was copying. Then I had to integrate all of this and incorporate it in my painting repertoire. This continues to be a memory problem for me since I try again and again to reconstruct those moments when I painted well and often don't succeed.

Unfortunately, these positive details were still dwarfed by what I considered my mistakes. But that negativity on my part was almost always alleviated by Joseph, who seemed to anticipate my frustration and know exactly where I was stumbling in the painting. He was able, with a few strokes, to demonstrate how to overcome it or modify the whole composition so that what seemed like an error looked natural and planned.

Joseph's solutions were as helpful as his praise. Once, I was working on a more complex landscape and having major problems

with it. Fen was watching me paint, turning away from her beautiful bird. She was fascinated with the landscapes I was doing and made me somewhat self-conscious, though I knew she wasn't admiring me so much as studying the painting's complexity. There were three levels in this particular work: a foreground of rocks and trees; a middle ground with small, tree-covered hills with a temple hidden among them; and a background of high mountains way off in the distance. I began the painting on the lower right and became lost in the rocks and trees. I had just gotten the hang of painting three different species of trees and was tree-painting obsessed at the time. When it became time to move to the middle ground, I faced an unanticipated problem. There was a little room for the hills and the temple but certainly none for the tall mountains. I had forgotten to consider proportion in planning my work. I just jumped in and started painting.

Proportion, balancing all of the elements in a work, has definitely been a painting problem for me. I make things too large or too small or forget the whole while working on the details. I expect that's been largely a consequence of occasionally feeling overwhelmed by all of the components that have to be considered when working in such a new media. Joseph understood my problems with my landscape, where the trees and rocks in the foreground made it impossible to include the temples or the high mountains in the distance. He suggested a solution. Paint the middle ground and forget the mountains. He said that would look good, and then with a piece of charcoal he outlined places on my rice paper where I could fit in the missing middle ground. At the beginning of the next session, I found a piece of charcoal at my painting place. The idea was to remember the whole while painting the particular.

Placement and proportion became especially important for me when I started painting landscapes that contained houses, temples, and people in them or that had large expanses of water filled with single-sail fishing boats. Here, proportion was everything. With one or two exceptions, none of the boats, people, or buildings were in the foreground. A person walking a mountain path and seen from a distance is tiny, a boat seen from a distance can hardly be portrayed in detail. At first glance, it's sometimes easy to miss a temple hidden in the trees halfway up a tree-studded mountain.

Joseph's teaching method doesn't include preliminary lessons. Even with the much more difficult landscapes, he presented paintings for me to copy and then watched as I proceeded, stepped in when I faced a problem, and simply showed me how to proceed by taking the brush and making one or two strokes that pushed the painting along. Each of these mini-lessons was valuable. I saw, in the context of an evolving painting, how things fit together. For example, one day I was painting three different kinds of trees in the foreground of a mountain landscape. Joseph came over and looked at my trees. He then said that they were too regular and symmetric, that trees in the real world don't grow the same on both sides, that I should paint more leaves on one side of the tree than on the other and look at trees to see how the leaves clustered. He implied that painting Chinese was not painting by numbers and staying in the lines, but creating a balance between regularity and irregularity, between yin and yang. It consisted of taming the contradiction between order and disorder, a balancing act that has to seem incomplete, like the text Monkey King brought back from China. The energy that resides in the painting comes from this moment of tension that never resolves itself. In the most satisfying painting, I've noticed that symmetry is indeed broken and there is some unresolved tension that makes the work come alive.

Sometimes I would make a large clumsy boat on a lake in the midst of towering mountains. The boat I was copying was tiny, was seen from a great distance, and looked as if it were moving in the wind. With a few strokes, Joseph would turn it into a larger two-master instead of a single-sail small boat; at other times, he might transform it into a rock in the midst of a lake. He illustrated how to work with the painting and never abandon it in frustration. This was a very important lesson to me, since I was ready to quit at the university prematurely and struggling with my paintings became a metaphor for struggling to preserve my program. I finally decided to make the best of what I had to work with at the university, complete the project, and move on to some new challenges just as I moved on to new paintings.

Fortunately, Judy and I went home to Point Arena every weekend, even though it is a four-hour drive from San Francisco. This gave us a chance to take long walks and gave me the chance to paint at home. There are two large ravens that live in the trees that surround our house. They come very close to the house when we put out scraps for our compost. The more I painted at home, the more I wanted the ravens to be in the landscape and so developed a signature for the paintings I did at home. There were several birds in one of the paintings I did with Joseph. They were far off in the distance, flying above the mountains. Actually, they were just one or two small brushstrokes indicating wings that when seen in the context of the painting clearly indicated birds. I decided to work three or four ravens into all of the landscapes I practiced when I was in the country as my signature, though I never tried to do that when painting at Joseph's. When I was at school, I was copying; when I was at home, I was elaborating on the traditional work I was doing.

One day in the middle of that semester, Joseph provided me with another signature to use to sign my painting. It consisted of three Chinese ideograms that he drew and interpreted for me.

The first ideogram meant "conspicuous" or "grand," the second "uncle," and the third "special." After I put them together and reordered them according to English syntax, they read, "special conspicuous granduncle," something that made me think of my relationship to the children. For several weeks, I signed all my paintings with my Chinese name and even went back to older paintings that I particularly liked and signed them with my three ideograms.

Joseph even suggested I think of a poem or saying that could fit with the painting and write it, in English, on the painting. Many classical Chinese paintings have calligraphed poems painted directly onto the rice paper. They are integral components of the whole. I tried this once or twice at home and found myself making a mess of the printing, so I abandoned the practice. This Chinese tradition of poetic enhancement of paintings is quite wonderful; it is as if you are hearing the voice of the poet while looking through the eyes of the painter.

At the end of the semester, Joseph surprised me again by

赫伯特

赫伯特

presenting me with a stamp of my name that he had carved out of a beautiful soft stone. He also presented me with a small porcelain container with soft red ink in it and explained that he gave these things to me so that I could sign my work in the traditional Chinese way. The time had come for me to stamp my name on my paintings. They were no longer practice exercises, but beginning paintings that had to be claimed and honored by the painter. I was humbled and delighted. I couldn't contain myself when I showed the stamp to Judy and practiced stamping my name dozens of times when I got home. It turned out the practice was necessary. Like everything else I was learning in painting Chinese, this could not be done casually. The art of stamping your name is precise and exact. It was very easy to have too much

or too little ink on the stamp, to press it too lightly or with too much pressure.

After receiving my name and stamp, I took landscape painting much more seriously because it showed Joseph's respect for my painting. I began to spend more time at the Asian Art Museum studying Chinese landscape painting. I also began to read about the history of the paintings and their relationship to different dynasties and their political and social struggles and successes. In class, I pushed myself harder and harder to paint well, to little result. Joseph noticed this and told me to listen more to my heart and relax my brushstrokes. It was crucial to work my way slowly into discovering myself as a painter and not try the unobtainable and seek to become a master through shortcuts. In fact, it was essential not to seek to become a master, but to paint and let whatever mastery emerged speak for itself.

I continued to paint landscapes during a short summer session and then spent the rest of the summer painting at home. I listened to Joseph and sketched trees, the ocean in many of its moods, the staggering rock faces on the shore, the river down the road from us, the pond outside the window of my study, the rock roses in front of our house, and the redwood trees that are everywhere on our land. Then I took my sketches and tried to turn them into Chinese paintings. It was fun—I practiced what I had learned, with a bit of my old impressionist style thrown in occasionally. If a painting of a tree didn't work, I'd turn it into an ant or a monster; oceans became green and red and purple, flowers had eyes and sometimes menacing teeth. There was no Joseph to hold me to the traditional mode. In a way, I regretted he wasn't there to support me and provide new skills and techniques. But I did enjoy being the wicked child, the bad student, for just a little while.

Most of my painting that summer was traditional, impression style, as Joseph called it. There were a few paintings I really liked, and most of all I liked the painting itself. It relaxed me at a time when I was grieving over the end of my program at the university and feeling that I could never again gather enough energy and will to develop a large-scale project from scratch. I felt selfish at indulging myself so much in painting, but Judy kept telling me that was foolish. It was okay to do some things just for their own sake—for no social benefit or monetary gain.

In the fall, I returned to San Francisco for another year, this time at Mission High School. I loved being in the context of a school again and was determined to make the best of the year. I didn't have the slightest idea what I would do after that, and this opened the door to periodic anxiety and sadness. Painting and Judy's support kept this from getting out of hand, and when we moved back to San Francisco for a final year, I registered for another semester at the Joseph Fine Arts School.

When young we heedlessly watch the mid-autumn moon,
Seeing this time as all other time.
With the coming of age respect has grown,
And we do not look lightly
Every time we raise the deep cup to celebrate the feast.

young as I wanted to be, or at least that I could live youthfully while getting older. And being taught by Joseph was such an important learning experience for me that I felt at that moment like an abandoned child. I loved being his student. I didn't want to break that magic and grow up again. Yet I obediently followed Joseph into the other room. My painting station was in a corner, not at the central table. I would be painting all alone.

On reflection, I have come to understand that being among the children and painting with Joseph was a way not merely of learning something new, but of growing up again. Though unspoken, I was allowing myself to be a child, a student, a learner in ways I had never been while growing up. It was indeed new to me to be free of criticism and pressure, of feeling inferior because I didn't get everything right. I remember in school in the Bronx I once came home with a report card that had all A's except for one A–. My father's response was to ask me what was wrong with me because I got the A–. None of that could happen with Joseph, and silly as it sounds, none of the other children at Joseph's could make fun of me as some of my elementary school friends did because my asthma made it difficult for me to compete in sports. In addition, I was learning what I loved rather than hiding behind a textbook and praying I got the answer the teacher expected of me. In my own teaching, I try to be the kind of teacher Joseph was for me, but I had never experienced being a pupil in my own class. I fought to create a wonderful, supportive learning environment for my students so that they would embrace learning instead of hate schooling. Now here I was experiencing it. It was a new childhood for me, much more precious than I realized when I was going through it. Now that it was being taken from me, I was disoriented. But if this adventure with painting Chinese, personal and spiritual as well as artistic, was to take me to another level of growth, I supposed it made sense to follow along wherever it led me. I was, after all, a student once more.

I waited at the table, feeling thoroughly depressed. After a while, Joseph and his wife, Janny, came over. Janny was to be my new teacher. This was totally unexpected. Up to that time, I was learning Joseph's version of impression painting, or *xieyi*, which was characterized by ink outlines and simple, bold strokes with little attention to intricate detail. It uses blue, gray, green, and red washes to create swatches of colors and a sense of energy and feeling in the work. Joseph told me it was perfectly suited to introducing painting, though it was difficult to master. However, he explained, it was time for me to learn more about what was traditionally called *gonbi* style, which is more formal, with fine, carefully controlled brushwork and close attention to details.

Over the course of my lessons, Joseph had said a number of times that Janny was a more distinguished painter than him and that her training was more traditional. I had noticed that at the central table in her teaching room there were only four students, one at each side. They were doing large, complex paintings. There was an older woman (it was even possible she was younger than me, but I still hadn't broken the habit of thinking of older people as "them" and excluding myself from the category) who was painting a large floral design with beautiful flowers and leaves and branches. Then there was a younger woman working on a detailed, elegant landscape that showed more skill than I dreamed of obtaining. I don't remember the other works that were in process in Janny's room, but the general impression was one of high skill and deep dedication. And what saddened me most was the image of people working alone on individual projects. I wondered how long I could put up with that and how strong my commitment to painting Chinese was without the children.

I didn't have the slightest idea what Janny (her Chinese name is Xiao Qin Huang) would be like as a teacher. In one of our conversations before class, she told me that when she was a little girl she really liked drawing and learned a great deal from her brother, who was an accomplished artist. During the time of the Cultural Revolution in China, she said, she stayed home instead of going to work in the factories or with farmers in the countryside. When she was in her early teens, through friends of the family, she became a student of some of the most distinguished calligraphers and traditional Chinese painters. These artists taught at home since the colleges weren't open. Joseph described them in the following way: "Her teachers are all famous in China. Chinese art history will show her teachers' names."

Janny told me that during those days, she painted at least eight hours per day. In 1975, she was required to go to a factory to work. She said that after dinner until midnight, she painted. I imagine it kept her motivated and full of hope during very difficult times. After the Cultural Revolution, she went to Jiang-Su Province Chinese Painting Academy, and during that period, she spent most of her time studying and copying the classical masters of Chinese painting. However, every year her class would take a trip to different parts of China to actually experience the landscapes that the masters painted. Then the students were encouraged to create their own versions of the landscapes they had seen and to develop their own styles and put their own personality into their work. The mix of formal and experiential learning that Janny described to me made complete sense. I have always wanted my students to become knowledgeable about technique and creative innovators but never encountered a systematic program that incorporated those seemingly contrary goals.

Janny made it clear to me that she teaches only strict classical Chinese style. Consequently, I knew that I would be taking on some difficult challenges and had to decide whether I wanted to devote myself to the painting in a more isolated social context. I went through the first class completing my last painting with Joseph, one that was waiting for me at my new easel. And I knew that when I got home, I'd have to have a long talk with Judy to think through how I felt about continuing painting.

When Judy picked me up after the lesson, she immediately noticed that something was wrong. Usually I'm ebullient, almost giddy, after a lesson. I chatter on about the children, about what Joseph showed me, and about how useful it was in helping me sort out what the future meant for both of us as I left the university tired, depressed, and feeling old, without any plans for the future. I could pretend that I was ready to begin again to the students in my program, but not to Judy. She knew how anxious I was and how much painting Chinese calmed me and provided a vehicle for thinking through life to dying and death. I don't know how she put up with all my obsessions, but we have been lucky, loving and supporting each other ever since we met over forty years ago.

I told her since I had to leave the children, I was also thinking about quitting painting. She said that children grow up, and growing up isn't that bad. I spent that evening thinking about Joseph and the children. I had to acknowledge that I couldn't stay in the beginners' class indefinitely. I knew the children didn't want to stay there forever but wanted to move on to more advanced painting. Though it was a resting place for me, I did have to grow beyond it. If this adventure for me was to be some secular version of being born again, I had to grow up. Perhaps continuing to paint with Janny would also become a source of strength. Certainly it would push my painting further.

I looked back at all of my paintings and did see growth. But I also became painfully aware of what I couldn't yet do. And I realized I didn't want to stop painting, but also that it was clear I couldn't do it by myself. It was not a matter of being able to develop mastery solely through personal exploration. I needed a teacher. Why not Janny? After all, I would still be going to Joseph's and be around, if not with, the beginners' class.

The next week I showed up a bit early, prepared my new painting place, and waited to see what Janny would give me to do. As the beginning students came in, new students I did not know, I felt like the big kid. It seemed ridiculous, but I was able to find pleasure growing up again in this new context, being old, acting young, and trying to balance the contradictions this implied. Yin and yang in my personal journey to the West.

LOOKING FOR CHANG: THE TAOIST
RECLUSE OF SOUTH STREAM
Everywhere along the path I followed,
On the moss
*   I saw the print of your wooden shoes.*
White clouds clung around your quiet islet,
Scented grasses blocked your idle door.
When rain passed,
*   I noticed the beauty of the pine trees;*
Following the hill path
*   I reached the stream's source.*
The flowers, the torrent, and thoughts of meditation
Composed one harmony—
*   There was no need of speech.*

—LIU CHANGQING

My first lesson with Janny began with her placing a complex, detailed landscape on my easel. Clearly, I was to copy it in the tradition of the school. Only I didn't have the slightest idea where to
begin. Janny sensed that, and after making her rounds with the
other students, she returned to my station. Typically, Joseph would
just indicate where to begin. Janny suggested I look closely at the
painting and then sketch out, with a piece of charcoal, the main
blocks in the painting. There were mountains in the distance, one
block; a group of low boulders, tree-covered mountains at the

middle-ground right; a valley in the middle-ground center; a group of small trees in the middle-ground right; and in the foreground, large trees on the left, high grass in the middle, and a pile of very large rocks with detailed surfaces on the right. This sounds like a cold, rational way to interpret a painting, but the whole was tied together by the artist. Every tree was bent just a bit by wind. There were four or five birds flying over the valley, and their wings showed them struggling with the air currents. The painting gave me a sense of an impending storm.

I sketched out the obvious blocks in the painting but didn't know where to begin. Janny must have noticed that I hesitated to put a stroke on the paper since she came back to me after her second round with the other students and indicated that a complex painting should be made in blocks and it's best to start in the foreground, on the right, if possible. I should do the rocks on the right and complete them before moving on to another part of the painting. Then she asked me to put another piece of rice paper on the table next to the one I would paint on and asked me for my inked brush. She proceeded to sketch an outline for the rocks and told me that it was best to start with the outline and then move to the details. Her outline was elegant, but as she pointed out, it was not an exact copy of the original. She caught the general shape and juxtaposition of the rocks, but it had a character that was hers. Then she handed me back the brush and suggested I try. In contrast with Joseph, she would never add anything to my work. She demonstrated what could be done and then let me do it. It was a step in creating greater independence in my work. I never saw a conflict between how Joseph helped me improve my work and how Janny went about doing the same thing. Both were supportive, always on the positive side, pointing out which places or even clusters of brushstrokes were effective and ignoring what didn't work.

After Janny moved on to another student (she was always moving around the room), I began to outline the rocks. My stroke was tentative. I ran out of ink halfway through the process, and after I re-inked my brush, the line became too broad and dark. However, the rocks didn't look that bad. I began to add some grass and small trees and tried to copy the wonderful graining of the original. I didn't come close to the dimensionality and volume of the original, but it looked more interesting than a lot of my previous work. One problem, which I still work on, is to control all of the shades of gray and black that are used by combining ink and water in different proportions. I know there are over ten distinguishable shades, and my work hardly uses half a dozen.

I kind of finished the rocks and decided to move to another part of the painting, the trees in the left foreground, before finishing the block where I began. Perhaps it was adolescent rebellion—after all, I was no longer in the beginners' class and still hadn't worked through missing painting with the children.

I practiced a bit over the next week and began to feel more comfortable with focusing on one part of a painting rather than moving all over the place as I pleased. It was clearly a matter of discipline and patience, but also of taking joy in the slow work of doing a detailed painting. This was new to me, not in my work in general, but I'd never done it in painting, and working with Joseph was paced more quickly, primarily because the paintings to be copied were much simpler. By the time of the next lesson,

I felt ready to return, listen carefully to Janny, and put aside my longing for childhood. After all, being an adolescent and stretching out could be fun.

Those days, I was teaching a writing class at Mission High School and working in the classrooms of teachers I admired. So adolescence was very much on my mind, especially because it was so rewarding to be teaching high school students again. My students were complex and aspired to be actors, writers, musicians, and poets. They reminded me of that fresh, joyful, sometimes dangerous longing that drives aspiring artists. I felt that same energy in my painting.

Class at Joseph's the next week turned out to be quite challenging. Janny had noticed that my rocks did not quite have the cracks and fissures and graining of the original, and she suggested I return to the first block and finish the inking with an attention to detail. She then drew on her sketch paper some techniques used to paint rocks. It was up to me to choose which one to use. There was no right or set way. To my surprise, I became absorbed in the details and sometimes overdid them. But I learned from my work with Joseph that I didn't have to make every stroke perfect and that it didn't make a difference what the outcome was. I just had to learn and practice and enjoy what I was doing. Disciplined, joyful learning with no stake other than the process itself was something that I'd forgotten over the past ten or fifteen years. I always had a program to run, a book or article to finish, a speech to make. It was life on the run, and I'm not sure how I managed to get almost everything done. However, the cumulative fatigue of working at that pace combined with getting older was becoming a burden, and I suspect that at times I was also becoming a burden to other people who cared about me. I always managed to make time for a private intimate life and to teach with pleasure, but it's hard to believe that the stress didn't communicate itself and affect others, particularly Judy. Sometimes I don't know how she managed to be so loving, supportive, and patient when I was often so distracted or exhausted.

I was settling into class with Janny, enjoying growing up all over again. That semester proceeded quietly, and I began to feel secure with my painting, though I still had considerable trouble with perfecting my technique and often felt lonely and isolated in my painting corner. One day I could control the brushes and ink, the next day there was too much or too little ink on the brush. I had to pay more attention to the brushes, to treat them more carefully and with greater respect. Joseph had told me that good brushes lasted for years, and I had gone through about a dozen brushes in just several years. The bristles would come out, or they wouldn't take a point. Sometimes when I was ready to give up on a brush, Joseph or Janny would use it as if it were new and fresh. I explained this frustration to Janny, and she suggested that I practice my strokes at home, not by painting anything, just practicing the strokes. I remembered that as a student Janny had worked at painting six to ten hours a day. I spent no more than an hour a day, and sometimes, when my life became complex, I skipped days at a time. Patience and practice would help. I needed to find a natural stroke that worked well for me within the tradition but had nothing to do with copying.

At that time I discovered, in a back room at the Chinese

bookstore I began to frequent, an intriguing book titled *Return to Painting* by Gao Xingjian. The cover had a reproduction of an ink-and-rice-paper painting that used at least a dozen shades of gray and black. There were no colors, just an amazing use of the white paper in relationship to the ink. And from what I could tell, the painting was modern. It was full of energy and mysterious. I had never seen a semiabstract, black, gray, and white ink-and-rice-paper painting before and didn't even know such painting existed.

I bought the book and had it gift-wrapped because I didn't want Joseph or Janny to see it, and I was on my way to Joseph's for a lesson. This was another bit of adolescent silliness, because on reflection my teachers would have known all about the book and most likely admired Gao Xingjian's work. It's just that I didn't want them to know that I felt a certain need for greater freedom in some of my painting, a need to go wild a bit and occasionally abandon traditional painting at home while pursuing more traditional forms in school. Of course they would have encouraged my experiments. For them, the more painting the better.

When I got home I took a closer look at Gao Xingjian's book. There was a gold medallion on the cover indicating that he had won the Nobel Prize in Literature in 2000. I felt a bit foolish not knowing who he was, but a short Internet search indicated that he was a novelist, short-story writer, and playwright as well as a painter. He also had a lot in common with Joseph and Janny: Born in the early 1940s, he went to the fields for reeducation during the Cultural Revolution and then became resident playwright at the People's Art Theater in Beijing. There his similarities with Janny and Joseph ended. His plays were called subversive, and he was put under surveillance. The play *The Other Shore* was banned in 1986, though it was performed in Taiwan and Hong Kong. In 1987, the same year Joseph and Janny came to the United States, he was allowed to travel abroad as a painter and settled in Paris, where he still lives. His criticism of the massacre at Tiananmen Square made it impossible for him to return to China.

Xingjian's work merges traditional Chinese ink-and-rice-paper painting with many techniques and feelings drawn from modern Western painting. I would call it Chinese ink painting abstract expressionism. In the works, one can make out birds, landscapes, and figures, all indicated in grays and blacks. They are highly personal and strike me as highly emotional. They embody this quote I found from his novel *Nocturnal Wanderer*: "Walk where your heart leads you, there are no restrictions and no burdens."

In the introduction to *Return to Painting*, there is a quote that I copied out and placed on the table where I paint at home:

Ink can be a veritable black hole, swallowing up all light and color. You know this, so you work the ink with water and come up with a spectrum of darkish hues.

Without water, ink has no vitality. Mixing the two, on the other hand, yields a million possibilities. But technique alone does not art make and playing with ink won't keep you happy. When you mix ink and water, you are mixing sentiment with spirit to attain a certain state of being.

That state of being, known to traditional Chinese, pertains to Eastern aesthetics. At its highest level it is known as kongling, *or "emptiness and spirituality." It is also an aesthetic judgement.*

They say it was achieved more than a thousand years ago, during the Tang Dynasty, by the poet Wang Wei, who was also a great painter.

Reading this astonished me once again about the unity of spirituality and painting in Chinese art. And here, once again I encountered, with greater understanding, emptiness on the Positive side. Monkey King was still with me.

At home, I began experimenting with ink and water, no color. I let myself go, drawing figures on the rice paper, surrounding them with multitoned rocks, creating water scenes that were all steel gray. In many cases, I just let my feelings follow the brush wherever it went.

Back at class, I tried to use some of the techniques Janny shared with me, but it was hard going. Despite the struggles, my brushstrokes were getting better, and I felt free to put something of myself into my copies. Of course, from the very start my copies were at the same time my originals. They always deviated from the original, sometimes in interesting ways. My work, for example, is not delicate no matter how I try. At the same time, this lack of delicacy lends it a certain forcefulness, often unintended, that Judy and my children find interesting. They are, of course, my first line of criticism, and for that matter my last line, as I have no intention of exhibiting or selling any of my work even if it gets competent enough to show. Painting landscapes is my form of meditation. It helps me understand myself and has, over the course of my lessons, become a source of strength. Working with Janny has challenged me in ways that the fun and excitement of

learning from Joseph and the children didn't. It lacks some of the exuberance I felt working with the children and has become serious as I work toward my own style.

However, painting wasn't and still is not my whole life. It just made my life richer and more focused. It made me less afraid of having nothing to do in the future, and since it is an ancient art form from a culture that honors older people, it began to provide me with a vision for the end of life, driven not by the fear of death or debilitation, but by ascent, by growth toward a mastery that can never be attained.

Painting Chinese enriched my political, educational, and personal life. It kept me from despair at losing my program at the University of San Francisco and not knowing what I might do next. It opened me up to thinking of moving back to my home in Point Arena for a while, resettling into the community, and writing instead of trying to be involved in educational struggles full-time. And it confirmed my belief that being on the side of the positive at a historical moment when the negative was ascendant, however painful and frustrating, was the only way I could live.

I enrolled for yet another semester, not very happy about my painting place in the corner of the room but eager to learn more from Janny and continue my explorations of the spiritual and historical dimensions of Chinese landscape painting. I decided to forget about adolescence. Growing up this second time seemed very attractive.

When I arrived for my first lesson of the new semester, I found that my painting place no longer existed. Instead, two carefully prepared tables facing each other were placed alongside the wall. I was to sit at the big table in the middle and paint alongside other, much more skilled painters. I was delighted.

At this time, I received an offer to spend a year as a visiting professor in the Education Department at Swarthmore College. I accepted, even though it meant a move to the East Coast for Judy and me. It was just a year, but I would have to give up my lessons for a while. The thought of it was painful. Nevertheless, a year away from the school might give me time to practice and absorb what I learned as well as visit many museums with extraordinary collections of classical Chinese landscape painting. At least that's how I rationalized it.

I didn't say anything to Janny or Joseph about the fact that this would be my last semester for a while—at least not at the beginning of the semester. But knowing that my time at the school was limited, I prepared to absorb as much as possible over the next few months. This probably was not wise, because it meant putting pressure on myself when the whole point of painting was to acquire the necessary skills to put spirit and love into the landscapes.

While I was musing about what it would be like without my painting lessons, the other students came in. Opposite me at the big table was an elderly woman who was working on a large tracing of an elaborate, sensitively colored display of flowers. Her rice paper must have been at least three feet by four feet. The painting she was tracing was very intricate, requiring delicate brushstrokes, carefully controlled colors, and an exact eye for detail. She was about a quarter done with the painting at the beginning of the semester. It was slow, steady, detailed work that required considerable skill and patience. I noticed whenever I passed by her station how pleased she was with this delicate work. She had a childlike radiance when she painted. Janny spent a lot of time with her, but since I don't know Mandarin their conversation was inaccessible to me. Clearly, some of it had to do with technique. Since I usually came to class early, I always made sure to look at the progress of her work. Everything was precise and beautiful. The flowers emerging from her paper were more vivid and alive than the ones on the reproduction she was copying. I knew I would never choose to do that kind of painting, but I admired it and marveled at the brush control necessary to make the flowers come alive.

The painting on my left couldn't have been more different, nor could the painter. He was a high school student dressed in hip-hop style. I could imagine him bopping down the street like a lot of the Chinese and Chinese American teenagers I passed on Clement Street on the way to my lesson. These kids were a delight, full of energy, funny as hell, playing around and flirting. Some of them spoke Mandarin or Cantonese, others English. Most common seemed a mix of languages, since I could understand the English nested into their Chinese phrases and sentences. The merchants on the streets knew them, kept an eye on them, may have been related to them. And even though they were strutting down the street in style, almost all of them were carrying heavy book bags. There was no contradiction between being an urban teenager and being a good student.

The teenager painting on my left didn't bop at Joseph's. Once he entered the school, I guessed his manner changed. He was quiet, respectful, very serious about traditional landscape painting, and very good at it. He was doing a mountain scene with craggy cliffs and steep drops into rock-strewn valleys. The work was all in black. He may have added colors the next semester. His work had soul and style. His angles were harsh, his renderings of the boulders and rock faces very grained and powerful. You could feel menace and danger there. And there was a hint of first-rate contemporary comic book illustration. His brush was steady and powerful, bold and true. I watched him throughout the semester and noticed how careful he was with drying the brush, mixing the inks, making sure that water was mixed with ink in many different proportions. I was embarrassed with my own, much more careless way of managing my painting environment and began to pay more attention to details, to treat my brushes with the kind of respect Joseph told me they deserved. I tried to talk to the boy while we painted, but he was too intent on his own work, and besides, the unspoken rule at the school was not to interfere with or comment on anyone else's work.

There was no one painting on my right, but there were two medium-size tables pushed together and turned into two painting positions facing each other. Two women who were friends or perhaps relatives worked at these tables and sometimes chatted quietly in Mandarin as they worked. One of the women was older and dressed quite modestly. The other was younger, had short-cut hair, and seemed to me to be very knowledgeable and sophisticated. She was painting at a table close to where I worked and went out of her way to be pleasant and friendly. Rules didn't seem to mean much to her, and she was treated by Janny with respect and familiarity. I felt the two women may have been friends with Janny and Joseph outside of the context of school.

Janny worked with both of them. It was the only time at the school that either Joseph or Janny worked with more than one student at a time. And the work was special. Neither of them was learning to paint. They were semiadvanced calligraphy students.

Joseph had told me that doing calligraphy was harder than painting and that if you make a little mistake, people know something is wrong. I didn't fully understand what he meant, and I certainly wasn't a connoisseur. In fact, I had paid little attention to it. In my experience, handwriting was a secondary skill, not a high art. Yet, as I've come to understand, the very form and grace of writing is an embodiment of and tribute to the meaning it conveys.

I've spoken to Janny about calligraphy recently, and according to her, "calligraphy is not about the Chinese character you paint. It's about the stroke. About how you turn the brush. The corner, you make a stroke up there, you turn too early, you turn too late, you make a stroke too long. There's composition to think about. In traditional Chinese painting, you have to spend a few years to learn calligraphy, then you start Chinese painting. But here, if we let kids like ten, seven, or eight years old do calligraphy for three years, they don't want to do it.

"Now, if you do a monkey, you make a beautiful monkey, maybe the head is too big or maybe the tail is too long, too fat. Or the legs too skinny, but it still looks like a monkey, and they feel they learned something. Then, later on, when they get to a certain level, they feel, oh, I need to learn calligraphy. When they feel like they need to learn, it is easy to teach them. You know, if you press them to do calligraphy, they cannot learn, it's hard to learn. Some kids, after a few years of painting, their parents and they themselves recognize that they need to learn calligraphy. The important thing is that they know calligraphy is important to them, because after they finish painting and sign their name, some students have a very beautiful painting, but when they sign their name, they say it's too ugly themselves. So they know they need to learn. That's the time. They know they want to learn, and then they use their heart to learn. Then you need to teach them."

The implication for me, too, was that calligraphy would be difficult. I was beginning to paint and thought I might never get to calligraphy. But I assumed that the women, my painting neighbors, were experienced painters and ready for calligraphy. And I also assumed they could read some Chinese characters, but I wasn't sure because over the semester I saw them give Janny a simple text in English that she translated into Chinese characters. Over the course of the semester, I watched the women's work and strained to find out how Janny was teaching them. They didn't seem to mind, but a glance from Janny always brought me back to my own work.

It was thrilling to be surrounded by such different types of painting, and during this second semester with Janny, I felt quite happy at the school.

My first challenge of the semester was a complex mountain landscape with a waterfall cascading down between two of the peaks. The foreground was a rocky grass shore on the side of the lake the waterfall poured into. There were also some small trees or shrubs along the shore. I decided to begin with the sides of the peak and then move on to the waterfall. Just as I put down my first stroke, Janny came up and reminded me to block out the scene and begin at the bottom, working my way up to the waterfall. She assured me it would still be there when I got ready to paint it. Janny's humor was always subtle, gentle, and pointed. It kept me focused on the whole, on the empty spaces as well as the painted ones. This was essential and was often negated by my not planning out the whole space. I would always steal from the white expanses in order to compensate for my bad planning, and that made a number of my paintings seem crowded, almost claustrophobic.

Joseph talked about white space in Chinese classical painting, and my understanding of classical Chinese landscape was further enriched by reading Gao Xingjian. In *Return to Painting*, he explained:

> *The pictorial surface always retains its flatness, whether the painting is in the "spirit writing" Xieyi style or the detailed and decorative Gongbihua genre. There is no real interest in transforming flatness into a direct visual space, and the relationship between what is near and what is far does not determine the viewing angle or establish the vanishing point. Yet for all that, the painting remains expressive. The use of blank spaces in the Xieyi style is even less constrained, and the interest in imitating visual experience nil. The void in traditional Chinese painting functions as a kind of psychological space. Those great white expanses are not there only to provide a space on which to write dedications but also to serve as a haven for the imagination and to cleanse the palate in preparation for the taste of ink. Covering every bit of the surface is completely taboo, because it leaves no place for the imagination to spread itself.*

Working with Janny, I began to think in terms of the whole of a landscape and at the same time study all of the details. For her, no rock or bush or shrub or tree was unimportant. Everything had to be done with attention, care, detail, and spirit. This was resonant with my personal "voyage to the West," with my Taoist intention to live on the positive side without hostility or anger to the negative people, but to understand the contradictions of life and struggle to create a peaceful harmony.

Sometimes when Janny demonstrated a leaf formation or a tree or bird for me, she painted quickly, but never without grace and elegance. I marveled at her mastery and decided to take what she was teaching me slowly. I could hardly keep up with her, or with my painting neighbors. Nevertheless, it became clear that I was internalizing the landscapes I was working on. I dreamed them, thought of them sometimes when I was taking a walk, and visualized details I intended to work on during my next lesson.

Taking just one hour-long lesson a week over a long period of time suited me very well. It gave me time to practice between lessons, live my nonpainting life, which was complex, and prepare psychically for that hour. Each week, it was as if I were going to a sacred place out of the usual space and time of my life and working my way toward an understanding of how to live the rest of my life. Judy understood this, and though we talked a lot about what was happening with my painting, she went out of her way to encourage me to pursue this adventure as silently and privately as it sometimes needed to be.

The importance of the growth I was achieving through my relation to the fine arts school and the philosophy and pedagogy practiced there was tested twice that semester by the deaths of friends, men younger than me. It is no exaggeration to say that they were both delayed victims of the Vietnam War. One, Leon, had contracted non-Hodgkin's lymphoma after repeated exposure to Agent Orange during the war. I knew him first through teaching one of his children and then by becoming friendly with his whole family. He had struggled for years to stay healthy but often was on the verge of breaking down physically. He was a very kind and spiritual man. On one weekend when Judy and I returned to Point Arena, we discovered that he had died.

I was overcome and found myself grasping for appropriate ways to console the remaining family. Given that I am not religious, the best I could do was help them honor the life he'd lived and dedicate myself once more to preventing such unnecessary waste of life.

To console myself, I retreated to painting, to portray him in an enormous landscape reaching the end of his journey high up on a mountain, free of the disease and at rest. This is a very small thing to do, perhaps futile, but it did remind me powerfully once again that my journey will end—not soon, perhaps, but in too little time. And it also provided me, perhaps selfishly, with an enormous appreciation for still being alive and on the journey. I still loved teaching, was in contact with students I'd taught over forty-five years, and began to become proud that they'd taken to calling me their grandfather. I embraced being old for the first time. I really wasn't a child among children anymore but felt I was still with them as they grew and matured. I wanted my journey to be deep and complex, to be joyful and full of companionship and love.

And I knew in order for this to happen, I had to let myself become old, an elder. I was lucky to be alive, learning, and with love and knowledge to share.

The death of Allen, soon after Leon's death, was devastating. He was a hardworking, kind, funny giant of a man whose son I had also taught. I got to know his family when our children went to elementary school together. Allen had seen combat in Vietnam and was unable to bear what he had been through. When he was sent back to the United States by the military, he was in shock and dysfunctional, a victim of what has been called Vietnam vets syndrome or, more recently, post-traumatic stress disorder. After a while, Allen was able to reconstruct his family life with the support of his wife and children. He did a lot of physical labor and was quite involved in local athletics. He was also part of a Vietnam vets support group. However, the effects of the trauma of war were always near the surface, and he had a near breakdown when the first Gulf war took place, reliving the horrors he had experienced in war. With support, he was able to stabilize himself and return to work after a short time. The same thing happened, except with greater intensity, with the breakout of the wars in Afghanistan and then Iraq. After that came Abu Ghraib and other horrors of war. He was tormented and depressed, though still able to function. One day, with no prior illness or notice, he died of a heart attack. Though it's hard to say with certainty what caused his death, there is no question that his experience of war had something to do with his dying.

Judy and I did what we could to support his family, but the whole thing was intolerable. The continuing pain visited upon ordinary people by others seems endless. I remembered that for

Buddhists, pain and suffering can be on the positive side, a way of moving toward enlightenment. But often I found the pain unredeemed and wondered whether this journey of mine would lead to submission to injustice and acceptance of passivity. However, it was clear to me that acceptance of the problems we all face in this troubling world did not mean a withdrawal from action, but much more a sensitive return to activism informed by the idea that you might not succeed and that for a while justice will not prevail but that you will provide a model that the next generation might refine and thereby succeed in ways you only dreamed of.

I couldn't paint for Allen, and when I returned to my next class at the fine arts school, I didn't know what I would do or say. I didn't even know how I would feel about being at Joseph's at all. For once I was a bit late to class, and all the other students were at work. Joseph came over to my place and said he was worried about me, and one of the women doing calligraphy said she was glad to see me and added that she liked my painting. Janny then came over and helped me set up my place. They must have known something was wrong. I just muttered something about having a hard time at work and began to paint. Their kind, authentic concern for me, conveyed gently and with great respect, drew me back into the landscape. I felt the same serenity and the usual silence of our working together that I did in the white spaces of classical Chinese landscapes.

Knowing that my lessons were going to end for a while after this semester, I was determined to learn as much as I could before I left for Swarthmore. Practice and patience yielded results, but whenever I tried to rush myself, I lost concentration and couldn't paint what I saw or embody my paintings with what I felt. Cramming is good only if you have to take an exam and then can forget what you learned once the ordeal is over. For internalizing learning, developing muscle memory, relating to the brush, and being able to translate technique into images, it is worthless.

For example, when I was working on a particularly detailed mountain face and improvising the details in an impressionist way, Janny came over to suggest the classical ways to grain a rock face that she had originally demonstrated for me. She then painted four of them on a piece of rice paper, translated their Chinese names into English for me, and explained their origin. For the first one, she sketched three examples of what she called "curling cloud." They consisted of a series of swirls and overlapping strokes that resembled clouds or clusters of clouds. The second was "fish scale" and consisted of an overlapping series of rounded bowl shapes that give the impression of being just what the name promised, fish scales. The third was "ox-hair" and consisted of a series of overlapping, slightly curved horizontal brushstrokes that resembled animal hair. The final one was "unraveled rope texture," which looked just as the name implied, a series of crisscrossing strands of a rope. These four traditional techniques, when used judiciously and rendered skillfully, give rock faces, boulders, and mountains a feel of depth, weight, and dimension.

After Janny moved on to another student, I tried all four on my landscape. Some looked good, others seemed to clutter up the space, and others just seemed out of place. I hadn't thought about what would work where or studied the original to see where one technique might be more effective than another. I was cramming them all in just to be sure I would be able to duplicate what she showed me. Fortunately, I took her sample sheet home with me, and I still refer to it when I paint. That sheet and a few other examples Janny painted for me have become a mini-textbook that now provides me with what could be called handwriting exercises. I say this because working next to the two women who were doing calligraphy made me acutely aware of how close painting is to calligraphy and how much of the skill of a fine calligrapher is transferable to a painting.

It took me a week of practice at home to become comfortable using these techniques, though I still have not mastered them. When there were three lessons left, I told Joseph and Janny that I would be going to teach in Pennsylvania for a year and wouldn't be able to take lessons during that period. It was a sad moment for me, and they expressed regrets. However, Joseph said, it was a good time to practice. I asked him and Janny if I could borrow some of the landscapes they would have otherwise given me so that I could, once removed, continue my lessons. They said no and explained that these reproductions of paintings were their curriculum and they needed them for the school. And Joseph explained, You can sketch what you see and then paint from the sketches. It would be good practice for seeing, thinking, drawing, and painting.

I wasn't so sure. For the most part, I had become dependent on being led by a classical painting. Of course, I had tried my hand at sketching and painting and at freehand painting from my imagination. But I found painting from the classics satisfying and secure. It was my meditation, and I didn't want to abandon it completely when I went to Pennsylvania. Over the last three weeks of the semester, I visited the Chinese bookstore down the block from

Joseph's and bought a number of illustrated books of Chinese classical painting, not like the ones designed for novice painters like me, which Joseph and Janny used as teaching tools, but the actual named and attributed classics. I also bought a five-volume set of black-and-white brush painting sample books, which contained dozens of examples of rocks, boats, mountains, people, birds, flowers, temples, bridges, and houses. The text was all in Chinese ideograms, so I couldn't understand what was being said about the illustrations, but they provided a textbook supplement to Janny's sketches.

I was desperately trying to prepare for my departure from the school. I worried that without an apartment in San Francisco (we were giving ours up), I might never return to the Joseph Fine Arts School and resume my lessons.

I worried that my efforts to continue growing as a painter might be fruitless without an organic and personal relation to Joseph and Janny and without access to their experience and the examples they provided. I knew I needed their insight into my work as I was actually making it and became resigned to the fact that it might end up becoming mechanical copying and not copying to understand the character and soul of the masters. I also remembered something Joseph had told me:

"There's a lot of books that talk about Chinese painting. But you read a book, you won't do Chinese painting, you cannot get the point, because you don't really know how to use a brush. Some people . . . When I opened the school, a lady came from Poland. She's so smart. She came with a notebook. Whatever you say, she writes down. She didn't practice here. After a period of time, she still cannot hold a brush. If you learn art, you look at how your teacher holds the brush, maybe just for five minutes. Even if you read a book for twelve hours, you do not understand. If you look at how the teacher use the brush, you get it. You learn something from the teacher."

I knew this was true, that you learn from the teacher. This does not negate the idea that you can learn through exploration and experimentation or discover a great deal by yourself. Student-centered education has a place in any creative learning program, but I've always added full frontal teaching to my encouragement of students' learning by doing. After all, I'm older than the students and know things they might find useful but might not discover by themselves. Through being Joseph and Janny's student, my respect for direct teaching has increased immeasurably. I am and have been a voluntary student of theirs and am proud of it. At least these were my thoughts the last few lessons before I would head to Point Arena for the summer and then off to Pennsylvania.

The last thing I did that final semester was participate in the student art show. Joseph framed one work of each student and hung them all as a gallery show after the last class. He even put a number of them in the window of the storefront. Next to each picture or ceramic vase or sculpture was a picture of the student and a short bio. Joseph framed one of my landscapes, and it was hung among all of the other students' works. My photo and bio were also tacked to the wall next to my framed painting. I was proud to be among the children, and Judy and a few of my friends who came to see the show were delighted by the quality and spirit of all the work on display.

I asked Joseph to frame an additional landscape for me, one I had painted while studying with him. I had put my heart into the painting and expressed in the grim colors and shapes of the

The movers left our apartment, and Judy and I followed after a last sad look around to check that we hadn't left anything behind. I knew we had to leave the city, but at that moment I felt some regret. It was too late to pull back from this latest adventure, so Judy and I got in the car and headed to Point Arena and a summer of rural living. In addition to carrying our personal documents and checkbooks, I took the brushes, paints, ink, and rice paper that I used at the Joseph Fine Arts School. I didn't want to be a day or two without them, just as I feel somewhat naked if I don't have a pen or two and a small notebook in my shirt pocket because I always want and need to write.

It was beautiful when we arrived in Point Arena, and the ravens that lived in the trees on our property were screeching. I took it as a welcome. The first few weeks home were taken up with unpacking. I transferred my painting tools to the painting station I had set up in my study, which is a two-room cottage about a hundred yards from the house. In the study are the books, toys, games, paintings, and tchotchkes that I've accumulated over forty years of teaching, writing, playing, and exploring. It's my child's garden of verses, my kindergarten.

My resolve was to paint every day for an hour. That seemed like a reasonable plan. There were no deadlines to meet, no classes to teach, no program to administer. Other than staying in touch with friends, a bit of writing, and remaining involved with progressive politics over the Internet and the telephone, I was free until Judy and I left for Pennsylvania in late August.

I started to paint using classical paintings from the books I had bought as models. Choosing a specific painting to copy was a

bit like a Rorschach test. I didn't go by period or date or by artist; I went by mood. If I was feeling *allègre*, I'd find a sunny, colorful painting, perhaps with a few people walking up a path in the mountain; if my mood was gray and grim, I could find a dark, fore-boding mountainscape with trees or bamboo blowing in the wind. I even tried my hand at painting people, insects, flowers, birds, and horses. Some of these experiments helped me open up my brush-work. I remembered what Joseph and Janny had shown me, visual-ized the way they taught me. And I took very good care of my tools, paying special attention to the brushes.

However, there was something missing in this work. It was becoming more and more Western, more impressionistic, and somewhat lazy. Without Joseph and Janny, I seemed to be pro-gressing a bit and painting for my own pleasure. But it was not disciplined enough and had very little energy. The classical land-scapes I tried to copy were way too difficult for me. I looked at them carefully, studied each detail, blocked out the whole, tried to mix the colors and capture the blacks and grays, but I came nowhere close to the originals. In retrospect, this close scrutiny of the masters was enormously valuable to me aesthetically. The more practiced my eye became, the more I came to love classical Chinese landscape. It really didn't make any difference that I couldn't copy it well or repaint it from memory. Simply spending time with a good reproduction and maybe sketching one rock or several trees, or trying to reproduce the movement of bamboo or the flight of birds in the distance, was pure pleasure. It removed me at least temporarily from the memories of the demise of my program at the University of San Francisco and from the anxiety of going to a new place across the country for an academic year. Also during the summer we had our annual reunion in Point Arena of students, now teachers, who had been part of the Center. It was wonderful. About thirty people came. They brought their own poems, stories about teaching, and musical instruments galore. It was a joyful weekend and reminded me how wonderful and creative many teachers are and how fruitful working under pressure can be.

Painting also grounded me. I did it for itself and to no conscious end or purpose other than the doing of it. I began to feel what was in my heart and to know I had to paint it.

However, growing old was still troubling me. What about life after next year? I had no plans, though I knew I couldn't commute from Point Arena to work in San Francisco or New York anymore. And there was no way I had the energy or inclination to begin a new program. I wasn't even sure I wanted to teach much more in my life, though I worked hard to prepare for Swarthmore, knowing that the students would energize me once classes began. I love teaching and enjoy presenting my students with information, puzzles, and readings they would not discover in most classrooms. And I love getting to know them, helping them articulate their dreams and develop the skills they'll need to become the people they want to be. I also love to learn from them. This has pervaded my work from the time I taught sixth grade in Harlem, my kindergarten and first-grade classes in Berkeley, and my postgraduate classes at universities. But I didn't know how much longer I could sustain the psychic and physical energy necessary to teach well. I was simply not as strong as I was at fifty or sixty.

We used a woodstove for heat in Point Arena, and each night I brought a wheelbarrow of wood from the stack on the side of the garage down to the house. During that summer, wheeling the wood, I had visions of Judy and me aging to the point where we could no longer get the wood to the house. Sometimes I imagined huddling under a blanket at dinnertime or spending hours carrying one log at a time to the living room. Recently, we had bought a propane heater for the house. We still used the woodstove a bit, but we made this propane compromise with aging.

Other thoughts popped into my mind. I had a writer friend who had just developed crippling arthritis and could not use her hands to write or type. Would my turn come someday? How would I get around that dilemma and keep writing to the end?

I think some of this "thinking through to the end," as I began to call it, was a consequence of having my work in San Francisco end prematurely and with an unpleasant conflict. But in any case, Judy and I would settle in Point Arena one day and have to make a fulfilling life there. After all, we had a library and a school, friends, and I even had former students whose children I could teach. We played with many ideas but were not sure what would happen when we returned from Swarthmore.

A number of the landscapes in the books I bought just before we returned to Point Arena were painted during the Tang dynasty, which dates from about AD 618 to 907. I also bought a book on Clement Street near Joseph's titled *300 Tang Poems*. It was published in Taiwan and is currently out of print. I didn't know anything about the Tang period at the time, but the book was beautiful. It was in Chinese and English, had original black-and-white ink illustrations done in classical style, and was well bound. It felt good when I picked it up to peruse. I am a sucker for a lovely book. After I bought it, I never explored it further. The book sat on a shelf, first in San Francisco and then in Point Arena.

One of the paintings I attempted to copy in Point Arena was a misty, mostly brown-and-gray landscape by Wang Wei entitled *Villa on Zhongnan Mountain*. It was hard to make out the villa, which was dwarfed by towering ragged peaks. The painting seemed melancholy to me, as if the painter were sad, lonely, and isolated. Of course, that was just conjecture combined with projection. Perhaps I was the one feeling sad, lonely, and isolated. It was just weeks ago that I could walk to Mission Street from our small house in Bernal Heights and wander around that bustling Latino community or drive to Clement and wander around an Asian one. I could go to Mission High School and be part of a multicultural, multinational world or walk to Courtland Street and be part of a progressive, predominantly white world. Point Arena felt like a retreat given that Judy and I would be leaving in a few months. Indeed, it was a willed and welcome retreat, but the memory of my city life was still alive. I immediately identified with Wang Wei's painting and read the text that accompanied it. It mentioned that in addition to being one of the great classical painters (unfortunately, most of his works have not survived or survive only through copies), he was one of the most famous Chinese poets. He lived from about 698 to 759, during the Tang dynasty. I remembered the Tang poetry book sitting on my shelf and began to read his poetry.

I do not pretend to be an expert on Chinese landscape painting, Tang history, or Chinese poetry. In fact, I can read the poetry only in English translation. This presents me with a dilemma when writing about both the poetry and the painting. I relate to Chinese classical landscape painting through what I learned at the Joseph Fine Arts School and have taught myself. My feeling for it is very personal, and it often works its way into my dreams, though I don't like to talk about it with anyone other than Judy, since my knowledge is so limited and my connection to it is so personal. Many of the essential meanings and metaphors embedded in the landscapes remain inaccessible to me, and I may misinterpret what is before me in the illustrations or the originals I encounter in museums.

The same is true with classical Chinese poetry. I have begun to understand some of what happened in China at the time the poems were written but clearly miss much of the context and meaning. I don't know the allusions, metaphors, people, events, or other poems they address themselves to or the complex religious and political circumstances referred to in the verse. This worries me, as it seems presumptuous to make Chinese classical painting and poetry so much a part of my life since I can neither read the original nor know all the subtle allusions contained in the work. Nevertheless, I continue to study the poems in translation and look at the paintings and let them speak to me, however partially that may be. There is value to informed humble amateurism. I don't ever expect to become an expert on Chinese art and poetry, but I certainly will take from the forms what I can and welcome their influence on my own work, thinking, and personal development.

One of the first Wang Wei poems I read was "Written at My Country Retreat by the River, After Heavy Rain." I selected the poem because Judy and I arrived back in Point Arena just after the rainy season in California ended. It spoke to me of my feelings about coming home to our wild and beautiful place.

> *Days of rain in the empty woods*
> *wavering chimney smoke—*
> *They are stewing vegetable and steaming millet*
> *to send to the eastern acres.*
> *Over the still flooded fields*
> *a white heron flies,*
> *In the leafy woods of summer*
> *pipes a golden oriole.*
>
> *I have practiced quietude in the mountains*
> *contemplating the "morning glory";*
> *For my simple meal under the pines*
> *I gather dewy ferns.*
> *An old countryman now, I've abandoned*
> *the struggle for gain—*
> *Why are those seagulls*
> *still suspicious of me?*

The last two lines reflected the tension I felt being back in Point Arena. The opposition between living in the country and being an activist in the city wasn't comfortable. I wondered if I'd really abandoned the old struggles that have characterized my life. More, I worried about whether I should abandon them, paint, and take to a more tranquil and removed life. I have always felt guilty about not having done enough to make the world a better place, and each time some small gain results from work I have participated in, larger obstacles arise and negate much of the progress. I learned through my reading and research that during Wang Wei's time, there was constant warfare in China and that he, like many other successful people at the court, relinquished his power and retreated to the mountains to become a hermit and spend his old age writing poetry, painting, and living within nature, harming no one. Somehow, I couldn't imagine myself that way, yet I also could not imagine myself being fully engaged again. I needed some time to grow, and Judy needed time to do her work in her studio rather than travel back and forth to San Francisco. We needed to take time for ourselves, something we have hardly ever done in the forty-five years we've been married.

During the summer, Judy and I took a daily walk—one day on the seashore, another through the woods or on a road overlooking dairy farms. On the walks, I discovered how much my perception of nature had been transformed by painting Chinese. I looked at the ocean as a force, alive and active. Trees had become individual beings, establishing their place in a crowded natural environment. I noticed how the redwoods stole the light from smaller trees and pushed them out of their groves. Raven colonies and swarms of turkey vultures became part of our daily lives as Judy and I watched them soar, swoop down for meals, and then sun themselves on fence posts near herds of dairy cows. All of this had been around me for over twenty years, but I hadn't seen it with such detail and specificity. I was fully there, living that moment and not distracted. I let the environment take hold of me rather than just walk through it. It was as if I'd had too much dust and dirt from the city coating my eyes in the past. That summer, I felt very much the same way I'd felt when I had my cataracts removed—the world suddenly became light, beautiful, and most of all more visible. Still, I felt guilty about enjoying this newness, this intimation of where my latest adventure might lead. I was carrying the competitive spirit with me, and it would clearly take time to become free to discover what I had to do with the rest of life. I realized, ironically, that this competitive spirit had to do with trying to do good and be progressive. Making money and having power to control others were not the only forms of competition. In the past, I'd wanted to be a good progressive, acknowledged by others, within leadership circles, and rewarded by public attention. All of the publicly praised aspects of my life faded, and the Tang poets I was reading illustrated a radical form of renunciation that seemed attractive but made me quite uneasy.

My painting over the summer reflected this ambivalence. I started adding paths to the foreground of my landscapes. For a while no one walked the paths, but just before Judy and I left for Swarthmore, I added a hermit with a walking stick on the path, at the far left-hand corner of the painting. He was just setting out on his journey to the mountains and had not even reached the foothills. The figure was tiny, and I had to use a thin brush, one I had bought at the bookstore on Clement since Joseph would never approve of my using such a brush. I'm sure that the hermit was me, wandering and wondering about the new adventures I would encounter during the next few years.

I couldn't use just one brush, and I practiced all of the things Joseph suggested to minimum avail. It was still a struggle, and

sometimes I cut corners by having many brushes instead of mastering one. However, the vision of one brush, mastered and being a companion for years, still inspires me.

My last painting before Judy and I left for Pennsylvania had the hermit reaching the crossroads with another road that led into the foothills of tall, ominous mountains. Distance from my lessons had led me to paint more from my heart and less from my mentors' instructions. As I packed my paints, brushes, ink, and rice paper to carry with me on the plane back east, I wondered whether it would be possible to sustain a year of painting without the support and encouragement of Joseph and Janny. I missed them in my life and my work. On the other hand, the idea of painting without the discipline I had at the school was a delightful challenge.

AUTUMN BEGINS
Autumn begins unnoticed. Nights slowly lengthen.
and little by little, clear wind turns colder and colder,

summer's blaze giving way. My thatch hut grows
   still.
At the bottom stair, in bunchgrass, lit dew shimmers.

—MENG HAO-JAN

Judy and I arrived at Swarthmore just as summer faded into autumn. The campus, located on the grounds of an arboretum, was gracious and well manicured. There were trees from all over the world, labeled for the unknowing and obviously pampered. Some of the trees were beginning to display their autumn colors. Judy and I had not experienced fall foliage or a cold winter in over twenty-five years and felt that the weather itself would be an adventure. The college had provided us with a furnished house and did everything possible to make us feel welcome and comfortable.

The first thing we did was look for places to work. It's a habit that has stood us in good stead over the years. We spend so much time together that it is important for each of us to have a private place where our different styles can be developed. My study is full of clutter, toys and figures and figurines and books piled all over the place. Judy's place is somewhat more austere, though it too has its creative disorder. At home, her studio is full of her metal found-sculptures and of scraps that will make up new works. She has several looms and a small office where she writes. In Swarthmore, we re-created miniversions of our working places at home.

I chose a small breakfast room off the kitchen, and she picked a study upstairs. The first thing I did in my tiny study was set up a painting place. Then came the computer and everything else. Painting took the place of honor, and in the first week, after doing some warm-up exercises and small sketches, I painted a mountain landscape. It is one of my favorites, and I had it framed. It hung in the living room in Swarthmore throughout the year, and I must have explained it at least fifty times to my students, who often came to our house for conferences or classes.

The landscape was all in browns and blacks, and the rocks were highly detailed, with some of the techniques Janny showed me but also with strokes that just came out spontaneously. The entire top of the painting, almost one-third of the whole, was clear white space, overwhelming, almost pressing down on the mountains. There are two main peaks. A waterfall cascades down between the peaks into a lake in the middle ground. In the foreground, there is a road winding across the paper with two forks angling diagonally off to the bottom of the page. At the fork are two figures, one smaller than the other. They have paused on their journey and are about to separate. The title I gave the work is *Teacher and Student at the Parting of Ways*. I had two partings in mind: one between me, the teacher, and the students in San Francisco I had worked with and loved; and the second between me, the student, and my teachers Joseph and Janny. It's not clear which roads will be taken, nor is it clear whether one or the other of them will leave the road and head into the mountains. It was the moment I was experiencing.

Swarthmore places a heavy emphasis on academic achievement, and most students I encountered there experienced constant stress to perform. A coffee mug I bought at the Swarthmore bookstore had the following quote: "Anywhere else it would have been an 'A' . . . really."

"Really."

I decided that my role during the time I spent at the college was to reduce stress, inspire learning, and get the students to play like children, even though the content I would present them was sophisticated and often challenging. I hoped the work they did would become part of an ongoing discourse about learning and teaching and that it would be fun and interesting. I wanted not to contribute to their anxieties, but to remind them, in a small way, how good it can feel to learn freely and willingly. I wanted to share, somewhat indirectly, the pleasure I had experienced at the Joseph Fine Arts School and with other master teachers I encountered in my life. I found myself enjoying the responsibility of being an elder rather than merely a visiting professor. It wasn't so bad; I felt like a grandfather learning to be in the presence of a newborn baby.

I also thought about Fen, Chen, and Hui Ying. It occurred to me that my students at Swarthmore, all conditioned to achieve on other people's terms, though quite creative and wonderful people, needed something fresh and new in their work and learning. They needed to smile the way the children did when they looked at their monkeys rather than worry about what grade their work would produce. What they needed was child work with sophisticated academic content. Just as I wandered about Clement Street to explore new places and ideas in San Francisco, I took to driving up and down the Baltimore Turnpike in Pennsylvania. One day I found Michael's Craft Store and decided to step in. I made my way through the aisles, just looking, waiting to be charmed, intrigued, surprised, or inspired. Many of the great inventors I have known depend upon serendipity. If you learn how to wander without a goal, keeping your mind open, new ideas come alive, old problems are resolved.

My first discovery at Michael's was in the aisle that sold everything from birdhouses to miniature furniture—all made in China. None of it was painted or decorated, and all of it was made of wood. I immediately thought of Joseph and Janny and their time in the art factories.

Over the past few years, I had been experimenting with "object lessons." I discovered Mark Twain's cabinet of teaching objects, which he developed for his own children. They were all tiny objects, like a pair of scissors about an inch and a half long, a miniature railroad locomotive, a toy woodstove about two inches high, and a bookcase with tiny, tiny books. Twain used them to spin out tales for children and motivate them to create their own stories.

The idea of lessons with everyday objects is secular in Twain's version but is derived from the church use of *object lessons,* which are designed to teach religious ideas through focusing on objects.

So before I left Michael's, I bought fifty small dollhouse wood cabinets at 99 cents each. The cabinets, whose doors opened, reminded me of the *offerendas* that young people in San Francisco, Los Angeles, New York, and Chicago created on the spots where friends had been shot down and killed. These offerings usually had photos, flowers, paintings, and objects that were shaped so they could tell a life story. My intention was to give each student in my class one of the cabinets and have them use it to represent events, persons, or things of significance in their lives. However, before giving students the cabinets, I decorated one myself. The top shelf had little plastic babies, the beginning of life; the middle one had Halloween fingernails, miniature books, and a tiny basketball, adolescence and youth; and the lowest shelf had some transparent skulls I bought at Michael's and a few more tiny babies, the end of life.

I think my cabinet was a summary of the voyage I was taking in my life through the vehicle of painting Chinese. It was so much fun getting back to provocative education, which is one of my specialties. And it helped me see my life and work as a whole and get a sense of the joy that could lie ahead even as I was aging.

I showed the students my work and gave them the cabinets. The assignment was to turn these unpainted wooden dollhouse cabinets into statements representing important things in their lives. With few exceptions, the results were superb, and at the end of the semester a number of students indicated to me that the exercise was one of the most interesting things they had done in years. There was a density to the students' work: paintings, photos, mementos of their childhood and growing up, representations of their joys and sorrows, details that, like Proust's madeleines, brought out memories. The students shared their work, and I did my best to tie their personal expressions into the images and imaginations and creativity of the young people they would be teaching in the future. I also hoped to help them develop a sense of the voyages they were about to embark on. As I was learning about my own voyage, it made sense to teach about life's voyaging. All of my work with students was energizing and rewarding to me.

There were many other assignments like this. I worked them in with the more academic readings, but frankly, I longed to return to Mission High School and my former students at the University of San Francisco. And, it goes without saying, I missed the Joseph Fine Arts School and my lessons.

Swarthmore had neither the urban wildness of San Francisco nor the natural wildness of Point Arena. Yet the fit for that year was okay for me, as I loved my teaching, though Judy didn't like being there. It provided an occasion for me to reflect on the future and have fun in the classroom and paint. As I painted, I had a chance to build landscapes and relate them to the whole of my life. For a while, my landscapes became peopled with poet hermits walking through the mountains, standing on top of mountains, wandering on the banks of streams. Occasionally, I would paint a woman with the hermit, not wanting to leave Judy out of my fantasy life. The paintings reminded me of the dream books I kept when I was in psychoanalysis during my early twenties. They also reminded me of the paintings Carl Jung analyzed in *Symbols of Transformation*. The difference was that there was no psychoanalysis or trauma involved, nor did I experience overwhelming anxiety or depression. I believe what took me to painting and the many thought experiments I made were the metaphysical and spiritual needs provoked by feelings of finitude.

Leaving San Francisco, spending a year at Swarthmore, and then not having the slightest idea what might happen other than a move back home to Point Arena was as intriguing as it was frightening. After all, I could still teach, write, and paint during the time left to me—fifteen, maybe twenty years.

It seemed such a short time. I had lost the conviction of seeing my ideals, dreams of a more just and equitable world, realized in my lifetime. However, I still cling to hope for a decent future beyond my lifetime, although I am sometimes weary of the struggle. Therefore, my first painting and thought experiments at Swarthmore were with trying on the life of a hermit writer-painter reaching out from Point Arena but being there in retreat.

I returned to reading Tang poetry and tried to think my way into the lives of some of those activists who withdrew from fully engaged lives in the midst of war and struggle in China. The Tang period (AD 618–907) was characterized by high culture and major disorder caused by continual warfare, not much different from our times. The hermit painters and poets (often the same people) withdrew with a sense of melancholy characterized by regrets and misery but also by ecstasy and a deep sensitivity to the rhythms of nature. Their actions were more extreme than any I had contemplated, and their despair was not like my wrestling with defining a future life. Yet certain poems like the following one written by the Tang poet Du Fu helped me imagine myself in the mountains with them, trying on a life of retreat:

CLIMBING A HEIGHT

A sharp wind,
the sky high,
gibbon's mournful screeching;
Blue islets,
white sands,
sea-birds wheeling.
Without cease
falling leaves
drift down with a whisper;
Without end
the Long River
washes endlessly by.

Miles from home,
mourning the autumn,
always a wanderer,

An old man,
   often sick
   I have climbed the height alone.
My hardships
   And bitter regrets
   have added frost to my temples:
In my unhappiness
   I push aside
   the cup of rough wine.

Not all of the poets were as bitter and disillusioned as Du Fu. Wei Ying-wu, in his "Cold Mountain" poems, often expressed contentment with withdrawal and unity with natural forces. It's as if he had found a way, through isolation and communion within nature, to transcend the pain and hopelessness that led him to retreat from human communal life in the first place.

COLD MOUNTAIN
I've lived out tens of thousands of years
on Cold Mountain. Given to the seasons,

I vanished among forests and cascades,
gazed into things so utterly themselves.

No one ventures up into all these cliffs
hidden forever in white mist and cloud.

It's just me, thin grass my sleeping mat
and azure heaven my comforting quilt:

happily pillowed on stone, I'm given to
heaven and earth changing on and on.

The extreme lives presented by these and other Tang poets intrigued me, while at the same time they did not appeal to me. But I've always found it useful to think my way into extremes in order to feel my way out of them. I can imagine being high in the mountains, sleeping on a mat, using a stone for a pillow, and extending that thought to wandering the hills during the morning and writing in the afternoon. It's the kind of life I could live even in Point Arena if I chose to be a wanderer. I could even paint it and actually did while I was in Swarthmore. But my feelings always took me down from the mountain and back to social engagement. I bounced back and forth from the hermit to the activist, holding the two of them in uneven tension.

I think I painted myself into a corner when I was at Swarthmore. I needed more technique, a painting environment, a school, in order to grow. I was beginning to repeat myself without improving. And the tensions I expressed in the painting were not resolvable at that time. I put off decisions about the future and, in painting, turned to flowers and trees. In Philadelphia, I found a store that sold Chinese art supplies and instruction books. One was lavishly illustrated by modern versions of traditional flower painting. They were characterized by swatches of color, impressions of branches and leaves, and occasionally birds in the distance. The technique used was one I had not encountered. It didn't use ink outlines. You began with the colors and directly rendered the flowers and plants and bushes without first outlining them. It was more like the intuitive and informal painting I was accustomed to doing in the past, before encountering classical Chinese landscape. I started painting one flower per sheet of rice paper. I used the Chinese equivalent of purple and a green I mixed up. It felt good to escape for a while from the mountains and the worries they embodied. Besides, some of them even looked good, and I had taught myself how to do them without a teacher. A bit of independence from the Joseph Fine Arts School was welcome, especially since I knew somewhere in my mind that my relationship with Joseph and Janny would likely be very different when we returned to California.

After a month of flowers, I began to concentrate on seascapes and to practice waves and the various representations of moving water in one of the books I brought with me to Swarthmore. I also studied photos I'd taken of the ocean off Point Arena in many of its moods. Little by little, I assembled them into mountain seascapes, views from the ocean looking toward the shore. Then I did some beachscapes before finding a need to return to the mountains, add people to my work, and get back to the question of What next? I took an inventory of what I'd learned since beginning painting Chinese and realized that I had grown in some surprising ways.

Painting Chinese provided me with a condensed second childhood, one I could grow through painlessly, stage by stage, guided by teachers who weren't particularly aware of my voyage. It was ironic: Joseph and Janny were teaching painting. I was trying to learn how to paint and be a good student but also follow my voyage through the stages of growth to become settled into old

age. Traveling from monkeys to hermit landscapes led me to understand the contradictions that drove my life. I have lived most of my life on the positive side, but the negative is always present. The sensibility of the Chinese painting and poetry that moves me enhances those contradictions: water versus rock, storm versus calm, war versus tranquillity, solitude versus companionship, love versus enmity. One landscape can hold all those opposites in tension, explicitly or by implication. Through painting, I came to articulate the contradictions in myself. In my life I have been a student and a teacher, a leader and a comrade, a hermit and an activist, a fighter and a pacifist. At times, my life has been driven by competition and the need for public attention. At other times, I've wished people would leave me alone. I love living in the natural world, but the wildness of the city is also rooted in my heart. Painting Chinese and my brush with the Tao has taught me that these contradictions are necessary and welcome. There is no final resolution to the contradictions, to the balance between the positive and negative and the striving toward wholeness. As Monkey King said, the holy books and all the sacred documents are and will forever remain incomplete.

Old age is a time to contemplate and understand the contradictions and find a way to live in harmony with one's spirit and conscience. Ultimately, this might be impossible, but having experience, being able to reflect on the past and grow through it, being able even to have a second childhood and grow up again on a more conscious level, and being able to put it into paint, music, words, and gestures seems to be the art of aging. There is no need to resolve everything. Death will take care of that.

couldn't pour the ink, wet a brush, even fill up my water glasses in preparation for painting. I even selected a scene to copy, but paralysis set in. My mind was empty of painting. All I saw was my study, stuffed with hundreds of books and figurines, the stuff of my life. Every object had a history and a story, so when I looked at them or picked them up, it was a way of meditating on my past. The ceilings had mildewed throughout what had turned out to be one of the rainiest years in the history of Northern California: eighty-three straight days of rain and the study was all but destroyed.

It wasn't just the mildew, mold, and leaks in the roof that affected me. It was the painting, poetry, and growing that happened over the past four years that led me to make one of the boldest moves I've ever made. This might seem a silly overexaggeration to many people, but my study was, short of Judy and our children, the most important thing in my life. Yet I couldn't paint or write in it anymore. I had to undo it and make it again, let it grow as I had grown. I needed a blank slate for my old age and for the work and play I hoped to do over the next ten or twenty years.

Leaving my study was like moving from New York to California. It was the end of one journey and the beginning of another—or was it? For weeks I sat amid the ruins of my fifty years of documents and books and illustrations preserved in order to be able to provide other people with a coherent archive of one person's engagement in school reform over half a century. However, the water and the mildew and the mold triumphed. I got to the business of rescuing what was redeemable and throwing out the poor, irretrievably damaged majority of my collection. This tested my hermit mentality, my sense of passing on a tradition, and the very center of my being. It dramatized to me how object centered I was and how much I needed to return to painting, writing, teaching, and re-centering myself. I guess it's all part of living with the Tao—the contradictions keep emerging and reemerging, and the struggle to delicately balance the negative and positive will be ended only by death. However, the Yiddish in me laughs at the serious presumptions of taking the Tao too seriously. As my father told me in Yiddish, "If you wish to get older, learn to suffer." I wish to get older.

Once again the problem of aging, being secular, somewhat insecure, and equally somewhat arrogant faced me—this time in the midst of the mildew and the mold. I wanted to cry, but Monkey King came to my rescue, and I laughed at myself and the fundamental absurdity of the situation. I asked myself, "What would Monkey King do" at this stage of the voyage? and I came up with the answer that he would make mischief and rebuild. That was my job, to stay creative and full of life and waste no grief, but just begin the reconstruction of a new study and get on with life.

It wasn't just Monkey King—Judy, in her calm and convincing way, just said, Let's get to cleaning and save what we can. No self-indulgence, just a lot of lifting and drying and throwing out objects and documents that are part of your history. She reminded me that this happens all the time, and a good cleaning out of objects and papers is often good for the soul.

I felt energized, renewing myself by letting go of all the specifics of my past. It is wonderful to be older and to have had enough experience to be able to throw things away and still remember them, condense them, write about them, paint them, and most of all convey them to my children through stories they

ACKNOWLEDGMENTS

I thank Wendy Weil, my agent; Joseph Zhuoqing Yan and Janny Xiao Qin Huang; my wife, Judy; my dear friend Mike Sahakian; and my son-in-law Jose Arenas, who did the line drawings in the book, and my daughter Erica, whose hands appear in those drawings. All of these people contributed to making this book possible. I also owe special thanks to my editor, Kathy Belden, who not only took a chance on getting this book published but who did a superb editing job. I have learned from her editing and honor the time, effort, and energy she put into helping me as I struggled to revise the text. Writing is a collective process and all of the people I have mentioned are my support group who make it possible to live through writing a book and seeing it to publication.

BIBLIOGRAPHY

Cameron, Allison S. *Chinese Painting Techniques.* Mineola: Dover, 1999. First published 1968 by E. Tuttle.

Gao Xingain. *Return to Painting.* New York: HarperCollins Perennial, 2002.

Herden, Innes, trans. *300 Tang Poems.* Taipai: Far East Book Company, 2000.

Hinton, David, trans. *Mountain Home: The Wilderness Poetry of Ancient China.* New York: New Directions, 2005.

Hsieh Ho. "Six Canons of Painting," in *Magic of the Brush,* edited by Kai-Yu Hsu and Catherine Wu. Taipei, Taiwan: Art Book Co. Ltd., 1982.

Lao Tzu. *Tao Te Ching.* Translated by John C. H. Wu. Boston: Shambhala, 1961.

Li Po. *The Work of Li Po, the Chinese Poet.* Translated by Shigeyoshi Obata. New York: Paragon Reprint Corp., 1965.

Shen Chou. Quoted in *Treasures of Asia: Chinese Painting* by James Cahill. Geneva: SKIRA, 1960.

Su T'ung-po. Quoted in *Zen Painting* by Yasuichi Awakawa. Tokyo: Kodansha International, 1970.

Van Briessen, Fritz. *The Way of the Brush.* Boston: Tuttle, 1998.

Wakeman, Frederic. Review of *Journey to the West* by Wu Cheng'en. *New York Review of Books* 27, no. 9 (1980).

Wu Cheng'en. *Journey to the West.* Translated by W. J. F Jenner. Beijing: Foreign Language Press, 1993.

A NOTE ON THE AUTHOR

Herbert Kohl is the author of more than forty books, including *36 Children*, *The Open Classroom*, *I Won't Learn from You*, and *Stupidity and Tears*. He coauthored two children's books with his wife, Judith, one of which, *A View from the Oak*, won the National Book Award for children's literature. He was the founder and first director of the Teachers' and Writers' Collaborative and established the Center for Teaching Excellence and Social Justice at the University of San Francisco. He was a senior fellow at the Open Society Institute, a part of the Soros Foundation Network, and currently he is writing, painting, and consulting at his home in Point Arena, California.